A
Single
Society

A Single Society

Alternatives to Urban Apartheid

DONALD CANTY

PRAEGER PUBLISHERS
New York • Washington • London

PRAEGER PUBLISHERS

111 Fourth Avenue, New York, N.Y. 10003, U.S.A.
5, Cromwell Place, London S.W.7, England
Published in the United States of America in 1969
by Praeger Publishers, Inc.

© 1969 by Praeger Publishers, Inc.

Library of Congress Catalog Card Number: 76-83331

Printed in the United States of America

6363

For Joan, who makes everything possible,
and for Kevin, Dennis, Mary, Hilary, Susan, and Brendan,
who will inherit the society we build.

Preface

Urban America's Information Center was established in 1967 to monitor the complex events and ideas that move a nation of cities. As its director (and editor of *City* magazine), watching this constant movement, I inescapably tried to sort out the events according to significance and relationship, one to another; to put the ideas in an ordering framework. This book is the result.

The sorting out and ordering are my own, and no blame should be placed upon Urban America. Yet the book would not have been possible if I had not been directing the Information Center. In particular, I would like to acknowledge the contributions of Urban America's Executive Vice-President, William L. Slayton, who has given full support and free reign to our inquiries, and the other editors of *City* magazine, from whose hard-gained information and insights I have borrowed shamelessly: Muriel Campaglia, Louise Campbell, Lois Craig, Lisa Hirsch, Simpson Lawson, Gail Miller, and Phyllis Myers. Mrs. Craig, in off hours, was research assistant for the book; it benefited greatly from her intelligence and judgment.

Gratitude also is due two friends whose immense knowledge made me realize, on arrival in Washington, how much I had to learn, and who helped me learn some of it: Harold Fleming of the Potomac Institute and John Feild of the U.S. Conference of Mayors. (They, too, should be absolved from responsibility for the book's conclusions.) Finally, I would like to thank the book's editor, Marian Wood, for so skillfully insisting that I said what I meant.

Summer, 1969
Washington, D.C.

Contents

A
Single
Society

Prologue

I find it astounding how comfortable we can be sitting atop a volcano. Perhaps a mile from where I write, on a white hill in Washington, are streets of such fear, such tension, such intense and frustrated rage that an eruption is eminently possible at any moment of the day or night. These same streets erupted just over a year ago, when the flowering trees outside the window were at about this same stage of beauty. The fire did not come near my hill, although the fear and tension did, spreading outward until it touched the farthest suburbs. Next time, I know, the fire could spread too, and it will take only the smallest spark for there to be a next time.

These things are on my mind more than most of my neighbors' because it is my profession to write about them. But they can be easily submerged beneath concern for my children's behavior, the condition of the beams beneath the front porch, status problems on the office staff. Were I not professionally involved, it would be possible to remove all reminders of the turbulence nearby simply by changing my route to work. I drive down 18th street, singed by the 1968 disorders, not without occasional apprehension. Many avoid 18th street.

It is natural to avoid disturbance. What is unnatural, even eerie, is the ease with which we as a nation can put out of mind the explosive core within each of our major cities. For a time we could say that we simply didn't know. Now, after five years of disorders, we remain able repeatedly to push the danger in the cities from national consciousness. We are like villagers for whom the rumble inside the mountain has be-

3

come part of the sound of daily life. We resume secure
routines between eruptions; after all, last time the fire stopped
short of reaching us.

It is also astounding to me how quiet the American conscience can be when not prodded. In the fearful streets across
the city, tens of thousands of people are being insulted and
damaged by the conditions of their lives, hour by hour. For
them, the living environment offered by the capital of the
earth's richest nation—a cliché, but that is the way it must be
said—is a deadly machine grinding at them until, for some,
not even anger remains. Hope, dignity, opportunity, decent
surroundings, self-regard—all become dust on these streets,
blown by constant winds of hate and violence. It is that bad.
I have seen the machine at work.

We as a nation don't want to know about it. We are end-
lessly ingenious in distracting and deluding ourselves. What
we can't ignore we explain away, passing comforting myths
back and forth until they become hallowed as truths. After
five years of disorders, that game is still being played, at levels
of society from the neighborhood barbershop to the White
House.

At the barbershop level, the favorite myth has been that
differences in energy, ambition, morals, and behavior go along
with differences in color. What can you expect from these
people, especially when they're stirred up by outside agitators?
Some social scientists have, in fact, acknowledged that there
are differences, though most insist that these are not inborn,
but are instead the product of a history of deprivation that
has produced an "underclass" among the urban blacks. Others
trace the turbulence on slum-ghetto streets to the fact they
are crowded with migrants from the rural South, who have
been poorly prepared for urban life, who have yet to learn the
city's ways; this, of course, cannot be considered the city's
fault. The common strain in this mythology is that the problem lies in the people of the slums and ghettos, not in the
conditions of their lives.

It is a comforting strain, because it relieves the rest of us of the trouble and expense of changing these conditions. One purpose of this book is to remove that comfort by showing that the slums and ghettos offer an environment so destructive, so dehumanizing as to make mere survival remarkable. The problem is not the people's misuse of the city; it is the city's, and the nation's, abuse of particular groups of people.

At the White House level, some myths have been carried over from the previous Administration and others have been newly introduced. Those inherited include the myth of progress—the blacks have never been better off, nor the subject of more governmental attention—and of the nation's fiscal incapacity to do more. Further steps, said Mr. Johnson and says Mr. Nixon, must await the end of war and the easing of inflation. To these Mr. Nixon has added the myths of the Forgotten Man (which says, in effect, that it's about time we listened to the hard-working, God-fearing majority in this country), of black self-determination (which argues that as the blacks say they want to do it themselves, let's let them), and of caution (which propounds that we need to know more about the situation before we can act).

This book argues the contrary. Wide gaps persist in the black and white experience of America, and expectations—quite legitimate expectations—are far outrunning progress. If the pace of the process of closing the gap continues to lag there will be explosions beyond any we have known. The nation can do what it must. It is not wealth but will, and an understanding of the danger, that is lacking.

In particular, the thesis of this book is that we know how to do much more than we have been willing to do. The tools of changing the conditions of slum-ghetto life, and seeing they are not bred again, are to be found in the myriad "demonstration" programs of the past two national administrations —programs that were tested, found to work, but never put to full use; in some near-unanimous recommendations of specialists in various branches of the urban business; and in common sense (the unremarkable proposition, for example, that more jobs mean less unemployment, and vice versa).

This thesis is implicit in the book's subtitle, which requires some explanation. Apartheid may seem too strong a word for either the present or prospective situation in urban America. Yet, as shall be seen, we live already in a state of *de facto* apartheid that, without too much change in our laws and practices, could one day become *de jure*. There are identifiable alternatives: The problem is not lack of knowledge about them, but lack of national will to change the trend toward further division and discord.

The focus of the book is on the slums and ghettos of the cities, where the nation's most pressing domestic problems—poverty, racial prejudice, governmental confusion, fiscal imbalance—converge with deadly and explosive force. For the rest of this century, the slums and ghettos will be, quite literally, the testing grounds of America's chosen ways of life and government. Their existence is a challenge to the propositions that a white society can be just and accepting to those of other colors; that a democratic, capitalist society can respond with compassion to the poor. If these propositions continue to go unsupported, the issue will become the survival of this society in its present form.

While the residents of these sections of the cities are coming to resent the terms "slum" and "ghetto," I fear that these terms remain tragically accurate. A slum is a place of physical decay and social disorganization; a ghetto is a place where people of a certain color, nationality, or religion are kept confined. To speak of eliminating the slums and ghettos does not mean bulldozing these neighborhoods and deporting their residents: It means eliminating decay and creating a human environment, working to cure social ills, and substituting choice for confinement. The residents increasingly are using the word "communities" to describe their parts of the cities. To eliminate the slums and ghettos is to turn this terminology into fact.

A similar point applies to the book's title, which is also its goal. A single society would not be one in which blacks are forbidden to live with blacks, Poles with Poles, Irish with Irish. It would not be a homogeneous society in which individual and group differences are considered evil and sameness good. The genius of America is pluralism; as stated on our coins (what more significant place to proclaim national purpose?), *E Pluribus Unum.*

There must be ways in which we are many, and proud of our differences, and ways in which we are one. But we are deficient in the oneness. To distinctions of class we have added the great dividing barrier of race, separating whites and nonwhites by places of residence, degrees of opportunity, and treatment under law. As long as the barrier remains, the nonwhites will not share equally in the rewards of society and we cannot claim to be one. A final thesis of this book is the familiar one about a house divided.

1

The

Near-

Great

Society

In the autumn of 1966, a committee of senators gathered for an extended colloquy on the problems of the cities.[1] The senators were a prestigious group: Abraham Ribicoff, Democrat of Connecticut and Secretary of Health, Education, and Welfare (HEW) under President Kennedy, was chairman; members included Joseph Clark, Democrat of Pennsylvania and, in the early 1950's, reform mayor of Philadelphia, and, from New York, the junior senator, Robert F. Kennedy, and his respected Republican senior colleague, Jacob Javits.

The first Administration witness was Robert C. Weaver, Secretary of Housing and Urban Development (HUD), whose very presence as the first Negro member of an American president's cabinet was evidence of progress. It was Secretary Weaver's task to open the hearings by telling what, up to then, Lyndon Johnson's Great Society had meant to the cities. He went about the task with obvious satisfaction.

President Johnson, he began, had, in 1965, delivered the first presidential message on the cities. The first federal department devoted to urban affairs had been established. "The

most comprehensive housing and urban development legislation in the history of the nation was enacted. . . . The antipoverty program was initiated. New aids to elementary and secondary education were provided. More effective and extensive programs for job training and placement were put into operation." In all, federal spending on urban problems had increased some 10 per cent a year between 1961 and 1964, and 20 per cent a year from 1964 to 1966.

Did the senators want to look back five-and-one-half years, over the entire Kennedy-Johnson record? In that time, $3.4 billion had been committed for urban renewal against $2 billion over the previous twelve years. Funds for 220,000 public-housing units had been reserved, loans of $275 million approved for housing for the elderly, grants of $169 million made for urban transportation. The list went on and on.

Did the senators want to look into the future? There were, at that moment, fourteen additional measures before Congress. One was the Demonstration Cities bill—eventually to become the Model Cities program—"a vital and bold new instrument to rebuild slum sections in American cities and to bring a new and better life to the people." There were bills creating the Teacher Corps, supporting fair housing, and providing more for the War on Poverty and mass transit—in all, a package that was to "help to build in our cities and towns an environment for man equal to the dignity of his highest aspirations." Said Weaver: "There is no deficiency of programs here. There is no lack of innovative proposals. There is no absence of compassion."

And yet, somehow, the senators were not satisfied. During the Weaver testimony, Robert Kennedy broke in sharply: "I don't know whether we delude ourselves, Mr. Secretary, just by spending so much time going over what we have done," said Kennedy. "It sounds on paper as if the problem is disappearing." Weaver, disclaiming any intention to make it sound that way, persisted nonetheless in his defense of the Administration's record. He was cut off again, this time by

Senator Ribicoff: "We have had all these programs and yet we keep slipping further and further behind," said Ribicoff. "We have reaped and are reaping a whirlwind of violence."

The Ribicoff Committee, in hearings that extended into 1967 and filled twenty volumes, heard from other cabinet members, from mayors, priests, residents of the ghettos, authors, sociologists, architects, businessmen, seers. Excepting the Administration spokesmen, those who testified were unanimous in general agreement with the Ribicoff thesis. The programs simply were not reaching the problems. Not nearly enough was being done, and what was being done, as often as not, was done the wrong way. There was no clear strategy, no long-term commitment, little understanding of how it was in the streets of the cities.

The Ribicoff Committee heard from those streets through Claude Brown, self-styled "manchild in the promised land" who had picked himself up from a budding criminal career in Harlem to write an eloquent book about it. Brown brought along Arthur Dunmeyer, who had spent half his thirty years in jail, had fathered an illegitimate daughter who was, at twelve, now giving him an illegitimate grandchild. ("We have but so many ways to express ourselves," said Dunmeyer quietly.) Asked about respect for law, Dunmeyer said: "Society has made this law to protect itself, not to protect this man in any way, and he doesn't recognize this law. Really, he doesn't recognize anything in society, because of this one particular thing: He sees there are no doors really open to him. Until these doors can be open to this man, there is going to be the same thing over and over again."

Asked if doors were beginning to open, Brown said that, so far, "all the white community has tried to do is placate, you know, just keep the niggers cool." Added Arthur Dunmeyer: "You can't just do it in one little spot. You have to go all over and look at every group, every situation for what it really is . . . and say, well, if I can straighten this out with these people, they can live with me. We can live together."

Harlem author Ralph Ellison also appeared before the committee. Said Ellison: "Now that so much money has been thrown into the neighborhood, supposedly, . . . the slum child feels very cynically that it is being drained off somehow in graft. He doesn't know. He doesn't have the information. I don't even have it. All he knows is that this promised alleviation of his condition isn't taking place."

Commented Senator Javits: "It isn't being drained off in graft, the millions that are being appropriated and are going into these areas. It just takes so many millions more than are being appropriated to really make a measurable dent."

The committee also heard from mayors and city officials, who had some ideas about the number of millions required. Mayor John Lindsay of New York, asked how much additional money his city would need for an all-out attack on its problems, hesitated, consulted his aides, and came out with the figure of $50 billion. The hearings almost broke up in despair. Mayor Jerome Cavanagh said Detroit could use perhaps $15 billion.

Mayor John Reading of Oakland and his redevelopment director, John B. Williams, offered several examples of community groups that had planned projects with high hopes only to find no money available, or had waited five years for something to happen in their neighborhoods while, as Williams said, "the dialogue between government agencies goes on and on." Mayor Reading had a blunt suggestion: "The point is," he said to the federal establishment in general, "quit making promises if you can't fulfill them." Mayor A. V. Sorensen testified that the 1966 rioting in his city of Omaha, Nebraska, "to a great degree was brought about by federal promises as regularly publicized in all the news media that failed to match federal performance." Author Ellison, calling the ghetto crisis "a crisis of optimism," apparently concurred.

Ribicoff and Kennedy tended to blame this particular crisis mainly on the federal administrators, but Javits was more inclusive. "I think we have been gravely at fault in the Congress and I think the country should know it," he said. "It is not just the cabinet officials and the Administration who may not have measured up to what could be their responsibility."

Local government came in for its share of blame in the person of Los Angeles Mayor Sam Yorty, who asked for it. "You don't know who comes into your city," said the mayor. "You can't identify them, and sometimes they are bitter and unskilled and bring with them some problems that they had in other areas." Robert Kennedy was unkind enough to point out that "85 per cent of the Watts people had been there five years or more" when the riots happened. Kennedy went on to characterize Watts as a slum, but Yorty disagreed, maintaining that Los Angeles had no slums "in the eastern sense."

Yet even the more responsible mayors acknowledged the limitations on their effectiveness, two with a candor that later made them prophets. "As much as we try, we really don't get down to the streets," Mayor Cavanagh told the committee nine months before Detroit's streets exploded in one of the nation's worst civil disorders. And Richard Lee of New Haven, the mayor's mayor whose city had found effective ways of using more federal urban renewal dollars per resident than any other city in the country, testified as follows: "New Haven has been referred to as a model city. If New Haven is a model city, it is a serious reflection on the condition of the cities of urban America. Because for everything we have done, and we have done a great deal, there is much, much more yet to do." New Haven was to experience its first civil disorder in the summer of 1967.

The Ribicoff hearings were something of a landmark. They represented the first wide-ranging congressional attempt to view the problems of the cities whole, rather than program-by-program and bill-by-bill. Like most investigative hearings, they were an attempt to reach the public mind. They came to be called the "urban crisis" hearings at a time when that term, far from being a cliché, was both a fresh and a frightening concept to most Americans. And they were held at a paradoxical moment in the brief and tangled history of the

Great Society: It was, as Secretary Weaver indicated, still in the process of assembly and it was already running out of gas.

Design and Delivery

The Great Society was born of the legendary legislative skills of Lyndon Johnson working out of the nation's grief at the loss of John Kennedy. "Let us continue," Johnson said as he took the office, and the nation and Congress were ready to respond. Six months later, Johnson stood before an audience at Ann Arbor, Michigan, and issued a further call: "The challenge of the next half century," he said, "is whether we have the wisdom to use our wealth, to enrich and elevate our national life, and to advance the quality of our American civilization. Your imagination, your initiative, and your indignation, will determine whether we build a society where progress is the servant of our needs, or a society where old values and new visions are buried under unbridled growth. For in your time we have the opportunity to move not only toward the rich society and the powerful society, but upward to the Great Society."

John Kennedy had brought new men and new ideas to the federal government. Strategically placed in the domestic departments and agencies were members of the first generation of federal officials to understand the emerging problems of the cities, the changing structure of poverty, the beginning, for the Negro, of a transition from concern with civil rights to a concern with social and economic equality. The Department of Defense was headed by a man determined to make it part of the civilian government, accountable, like other parts, for what it spent. Installed in the highest policy-making councils were practitioners of the "new economics" bent on prosperity through growth.

John Kennedy and these men had little success with their ideas in the halls of Congress. But with the assassination, Lyndon Johnson inherited enormous political capital, and he renewed it overwhelmingly in the 1964 presidential and con-

gressional elections. Johnson, the master legislative tech-
nician, had in the Eighty-ninth a Congress that felt his mandate to finish what John Kennedy had wanted to begin.

Johnson also had a great deal of money to work with. The
new economics were proving out; the nation had entered a
time of unprecedented prosperity. The great, flexible vacuum
cleaner of the federal income tax was bringing in so much revenue that Johnson could talk *at one and the same time* of tax
reduction, new wars on poverty, and budget surpluses. Even
as involvement in Vietnam grew, so did the Gross National
Product, producing further budget dividends that convinced
the President, for a time, that he could buy both guns and
butter.

It was in this period of political and budgetary riches that
the Great Society was designed. Ideas generated by the bright
assistant secretaries, special assistants, and consultants, by the
task forces of academics and specialists, became programs. If
the processes of congressional and Budget Bureau review were
not suspended, they at least temporarily lost some of their
characteristic rigor. The victories did not come automatically,
nor always easily, but they came—in education, in aid to the
poor and the unemployed, in civil rights, in housing and community development.

The process by which the ideas were assembled is itself
revealing. Two participants, James Sundquist[2] and John C.
Donovan,[3] have written accounts of how the War on Poverty
—the first major Great Society program to have the LBJ
brand—was put together. The offices of government were
scoured for promising concepts: from the President's Committee on Juvenile Delinquency and Youth Crime and Ford
Foundation experiments, the ideas of community action and
direct participation by the poor; from a Labor Department
youth employment program pending in Congress, the Job
Corps; from a national service corps program stalled in the
House, "Volunteers for America" (later, VISTA); from a
Small Business Administration experiment in Philadelphia,
a loan program for entrepreneurs in disadvantaged urban

neighborhoods; and so on. Sargent Shriver and his aides searched, stirred, mixed, and, in a two-and-a-half month period put together the Economic Opportunity Act of 1964, the basic War on Poverty legislation. The White House later released "a partial list" of those Mr. Shriver had consulted; it contained 137 names.

Later, the Model Cities program went through a similar gestation. It was conceived by a White House task force dominated by academics and other urban generalists and it contained many of their then current notions of what urban programs should be. The emphasis was on coordination of virtually all available programs, not just those in HUD, for a concerted attack on the full range of problems found in selected slums and ghettos. The attack was to be financed through an intricate formula involving both specific program funds and unearmarked "bonus" grants. The effect of this formula was that the cities were to add up their individual program needs, submit the figure to the federal government, and then receive a bonus in the form of a block grant, which they were to spend pretty much as they pleased within the over-all Model Cities plan.

A high official of the Model Cities program, asked how such a complex idea made its way into federal law, responded simply, "I don't think the President or Congress ever really understood it." Donovan makes a similar point about the War on Poverty, at least in respect to early comprehension of the political dynamite inherent in "maximum feasible participation" of the poor. In Donovan's view, the President was able to launch this particular war "almost too easily": It was possible, in the early days of the Great Society, "to enact and to fund major new domestic programs without generating a great deal of public excitement about them and without encountering a great deal of political pressure for or against them."

By 1966, when the Model Cities program was introduced and the Ribicoff hearings began, it was no longer so easy. It seems, in retrospect, a fateful and transitional year. On a march in Mississippi, Stokely Carmichael raised the cry "Black Power!"; it became, on the spot, a chant and, later, a movement away from traditional civil rights goals and tactics and toward militancy. Vietnam had become a full-scale war, driving a wedge of divisiveness through the country, taking increasing sums of money, pushing prices to new inflationary levels. In November of 1966, America turned out to elect the Ninetieth Congress in a mood of fear, resentment, and resistance.

Even the Eighty-ninth—"the greatest Congress in history," Lyndon Johnson called it, and not without justification—had grown balky toward the end. Model Cities only made it by an incredible series of hairbreadth votes and after a lobbying effort unprecedented for urban legislation. Other programs such as rent supplements, passed in the golden days, were left unfunded or sharply cut back. The War on Poverty barely survived congressional efforts to rewrite its mandate and reduce its funds, and was never the same thereafter.

The most common explanation for this disarray was the shift of national and presidential attention to the war in Vietnam. The impact of this war on American life is hard to overestimate; it has exacted an enormous price not only in terms of money but also in terms of less-tangible matters of temper and spirit, and, as such, it has made every act of national will more difficult. But it was more than war that did in the Great Society.

The oratory of its early days was eloquent, extravagant, and tinged with black. Every new urban program, whatever its scale, promised a new dawn for the American city. Secretary Weaver's testimony before the Ribicoff Committee was typical in content, if more measured in tone: This Administration was doing more for the cities, the poor, and the minorities than any in history, and it wanted the nation to damn well know it. The minorities, inescapably, turned up frequently in the description of urban problems that preceded the unveiling of each new program.

It is only in retrospect that the full extent of the mischief done by such oratory has become evident. Untold millions of white Americans came out of the early years of the Great Society convinced that untold millions of their tax dollars were being poured into the cities—most of it for the blacks; yet, the blacks were responding at best with ingratitude, at worst with violence. When the costs of war and inflation struck the economy, these people and their congressmen took a long, negative look at the Great Society programs. Small wonder, since these programs had been enacted without a strong, specific national commitment behind them—at a time, in fact, when the nation had scant understanding that anything was wrong in the cities. The price of the early, easy victories was being paid.

The blacks, meanwhile, were deep into Ellison's "crisis of confidence." They were listening to the oratory too and they could see, first hand, the gap between promise and performance. They had come out of the postwar civil rights struggles confident and determined, only to find, moving North in search of social progress, barriers at once less visible and more implacable. Donovan recalls how Sargent Shriver, in 1966, was driven from the platform of a poverty warriors' convention by shouts of "You're lying!" and "Stop listening to him!" from militants in the ranks of the poor themselves. Shriver was hurt and astonished. Jack Conway, the organizer of the convention and Shriver's former deputy, later told *The New York Times:* "He was trying to overwhelm them with success statistics. They released their anger and deepest frustrations at not seeing results." It was not the last such confrontation.

Finally, there were signs that the Great Society was no longer as close as before to the heart of its leader. Again, war was an enormous burden on the President's attention, but some of these signs came before Vietnam escalated into war. They began to appear, in fact, just after the first of the major civil disorders hit, in Watts.

In June of 1965, less than two months before Watts, Johnson delivered an address at Howard University that marked a high point both in presidential understanding of the condition of the urban Negro and in the Administration's apparent determination to act. Freedom, said the President, is not enough. Nor is it enough "just to open the gates of opportunity. All our citizens must have the ability to walk through the gates. This is the next and the most profound stage of the battle for civil rights." Johnson then went through a detailed and perceptive analysis of social and economic problems afflicting American Negroes and concluded by announcing that a White House conference—"To Fulfill These Rights"—would be held in the fall. The purpose of the conference, he said, would be to help the Negroes move "beyond opportunity to achievement."

It was the last such address by President Johnson. The fall conference was postponed until June, 1966, when it was conducted without excessive presidential involvement. In the November congressional elections, the Republicans picked up forty-seven House seats in a campaign that centered on crime and inflation. (In a remark typical of 1966 campaign oratory, House minority leader Gerald Ford asked rhetorically, "How long are we going to abdicate law and order— the backbone of any civilization—in favor of a soft social theory that the man who heaves a brick through your window or tosses a fire bomb into your car is simply the misunderstood and underprivileged product of a broken home?")

As 1967 began, the presidential message on the cities was replaced with one on "urban and rural poverty." And when Newark and Detroit erupted, the President's response was not one to inspire understanding. The night he sent troops into Detroit, after a messy political skirmish with Republican Governor George Romney, he appeared on television backed by the Secretary of Defense and members of the military; those cabinet officers having responsibility for urban problems were nowhere in sight. The President's words did not deal with the causes of rioting, only with the need for forceful response.

The Urban Coalition, made up of a prestigious body of national leaders, was formed just after Detroit; in late August, on three weeks notice, 1,200 people from all segments of urban life came to Washington to join its call for priority attention to the conditions that had brought about civil disorder. It received not a word of encouragement from the White House.

The 1968 State of the Union message announced a sturdy new housing program, genuinely innovative, but the President saved his strongest words—and received his most enthusiastic applause—for a warning about crime and violence in the streets. In March, the report of the National Advisory Commission on Civil Disorders (the Kerner commission) was released to thunderous Administration silence: The President, in his first—and almost his only—public comment, recommended to a group of businessmen that they read it; he did not recommend that Congress do likewise, much less act upon it. In April, after the assassination of Martin Luther King, he won from Congress passage of a respectable federal fair-housing law, to general surprise, but, in return, dropped his announced intention of summoning congressional action on a wide new range of urban measures. And that was just about that for the Great Society.

Mixed Legacy

The Great Society was left half-designed and considerably less than half-fed. So-called demonstration and pilot programs proved themselves, but were either left at pilot-scale or discarded. After the 1967 riots, the Civil Disorders Commission[4] undertook a study of the impact of federal programs on Detroit, New Haven, and Newark, three cities that knew how to turn the federal faucet and yet were riot torn. This is what it found:

During the first nine months of 1967, Detroit received $19.6 million in federal job-training funds under twenty-two separate programs, which served half of the unemployed. And the unemployed, as the commission itself pointed out, are only a fraction of those with serious job problems—the underemployed, those able to find only part-time work or earning less than poverty-level wages, are more than twice as numerous. In the same period, New Haven received $2.1 million in federal job-training funds, which reached less than a third of the unemployed. In the first six months of 1967, Newark received $2.6 million, which went to train less than 20 per cent of the unemployed.

The commission focused its study of educational aid to the three cities in the 1967–68 school year on two federal programs: Title I assistance to schools with heavy concentrations of poor children; and Adult Basic Education assistance for teaching the illiterate to read. Detroit received $11.2 million in Title I funds, which assisted 31 per cent of the eligible students; Newark, $4 million and 72 per cent; New Haven, $992,000 and 40 per cent. In Detroit, Adult Basic Education funds reached 2 per cent of those eligible; in Newark, 6 per cent; in New Haven, 4 per cent. Lumping together all federal aids to education in the three cities, the commission found that, in Detroit, they added only about 10 per cent to state and local expenditures; in Newark, 11 per cent; in New Haven, 7 per cent.

In housing, the commission measured the impact of all federal programs designed to help shelter low-income families, and went back into the 1950's for its starting points (availability of records varied city by city). In Detroit, 758 low-income housing units had been built with federal help since 1956, which was 2 per cent of the present number of substandard housing units in the city. But, since 1960, some 8,000 low-income units had been demolished for urban renewal. In Newark, the score was 3,760 units built since 1959, or 16 per cent of the substandard units; 12,000 families had been displaced during the same period by public landtaking for urban renewal, public housing, and highways. In New Haven, the total was 951 units built since 1952, or 14 per

cent of the substandard units; since 1956, 6,500 units had been demolished, to make way for urban renewal or highways.

In welfare, federal aid to Detroit totalled $48.2 million and helped 19 per cent of the poor in fiscal 1967; in Newark, $15 million helped 54 per cent; in New Haven, $3.9 million helped 40 per cent. In the same year, the community-action programs of the War on Poverty, totalled together, provided $35 for each poor person in Detroit, $21 in Newark, and $72 in New Haven.

In all, the median proportion of those in need who were helped *at all* by federal money in the five programs was 33 per cent. To what extent even these 33 per cent were helped was measured only in the case of the community-action programs, and the figures hardly indicate that their lives were changed. If the federal money was pouring into the ghettos of these three cities, it was hardly noticeable from the streets.

There is considerable historic irony to the last years of Johnson's Great Society. It had accomplished more for the cities than any previous Administration, more by far. Yet it— and Johnson—had faltered just when it was becoming obvious how much more had to be done: how much was needed, was expected, was, by the end, being demanded. The Great Society was frustrated in part by Vietnam—although more actually was spent on cities after Vietnam became a war than before—but perhaps in larger part by the deepening national division in interpreting the civil disorders.

The way toward healing this division would have been for Lyndon Johnson to offer, with all the persuasiveness of the presidency, an interpretation of his own—to lead the nation toward an understanding of the nature and causes of urban conflict and, through such understanding, to a commitment to urban change. The Howard University speech should have been the beginning of a new kind of presidential oratory about the cities. Instead, from that time on, Johnson tried to fashion a message for both sides. To the concerned, he spoke in numbers, proposing this many jobs, that many housing units.

To the fearful and resentful, he spoke in phrases that made no clear differentiation by cause or motivation between kinds of urban violence.

The nation thus emerged from the Johnson years fed up with civil strife, resistant to hearing about, much less attending to, the problems of the slums and ghettos. The problems remain, as does the potential for further division and disorder.

2

Where

It's

At

The slums and ghettos, in their present explosive form, were by-products of a new pattern of national life created since World War II. The pattern was not really designed. Instead it was shaped by the coalescence of countless individual preferences for places and life-styles. It was helped into being by public policies and by the two great forces of postwar national life, prosperity and mobility.

The pattern is metropolitan. The place where most Americans now live is called metropolis, defined as a city of 50,000 or more population and its more or less dependent suburbs. There are now 231 metropolitan areas in the nation, covering some 9 per cent of the land, containing two-thirds of the population. The life-style within them is unlike anything seen in previous history.

For metropolitan America seems to be achieving the unprecedented: It is becoming urbanized without becoming citified, as political scientist Daniel J. Elazar has pointed out.[1] Metropolis provides most of the economic and communications benefits of urbanization. At the same time, it permits millions of Americans to live at the low densities, and amid the greenery, that they evidently prefer to urban concentra-

tion. Postwar prosperity has allowed them to realize this preference.

Certainly, metropolis is unlike the classic cities of western civilization: Athens, Rome, the capitals of the European continent. They were centralized in structure and function, the marketplaces as well as the capitals. The cities of metropolis, Elazar points out, are more like those of Biblical times. They are focal points, but they and their surroundings are thoroughly interdependent. "From the first," he says, "the American city was really part of a larger geographic entity rather than a self-centered community, even in its economic purposes."

This interdependency has grown in postwar years. Many of the functions of the classic city, notably including those of marketing, have been spread across the metropolitan landscape. The American city remains the managerial core—the skyscraper, as Elazar notes, having replaced the Biblical tower—and the center of some forms of production (notably of clothing and publications). But the city is not the only focal point of metropolis.

The growth of metropolis throughout this century, in fact, has been increasingly in the suburbs. From 1900 to 1940, the suburbs accounted for 40 per cent of the nation's total population increase; in the 1940's, half; in the 1950's, two-thirds. By the 1960's, the core cities had stopped growing altogether, and the suburbs had attained a majority of metropolitan population. In mid-1968, there were 68.1 million Americans living in the suburbs and 57.6 million in the central cities. The suburbs were expanding at the rate of 750,000 people and 1 million square miles a year.

There were thus two aspects to the great postwar shifts in America's population: one, an intensification of the movement from rural areas to a new kind of spreading supercity called metropolis; the other, an even greater intensification of the movement outward from the city core. Both might represent a form of progress, except for a single fact. Many of those who came to metropolis were black and poor and they settled

in the core. Nearly all of those who left for the suburbs were white and at least moderately well-to-do. Part of the new metropolitan pattern of national life, then, is a, pattern of intractable racial and class division.

Most of the blacks, 3 million in all, came from the South to the North and West, from the land to the city. Some came out of fear, some from aversion to a social system that had made them chattels, others purely out of aspiration for a better life than could be scratched from the hard land or expected from its owner. And some came out of the immediate prospect of starvation: The rural south, in the midst of a revolution in the technology of agriculture, no longer had to be concerned about feeding its hands. It had machines.

From a distance, the city looked to the black man like freedom, like opportunity. Stories came back that friends and relatives in the city had cars, had clothes, enough to eat, so when the time came, he followed. But when he got to the city, he found frustration. He found, for example, that the only places he could live were in the worst parts of the city. He found the same hard look on white faces. And he found that jobs and honest money were not all that easy to get.

The jobs, in fact, were leaving the city just as he arrived. They, too, were going to the suburbs, where there was open land to build new stores and factories. This economic out-migration was measured by the Labor Department by counting the valuation of nonresidential building permits issued in the years 1954–65, when the trend was fully established.[2] Nearly half of the total was in the suburbs, including 53 per cent of the new stores by valuation and 63 per cent of the industrial buildings. The department pointed out that the greatest increase was in precisely those kinds of businesses and institutions in which the unskilled could most easily find work. The supply of new jobs at the entry level, those requiring simple training or none at all, was out in the suburbs. The need was in the city.

The dispersion of job opportunities, of course, was one reason whites were leaving the city. A cycle of economic develop-

ment was created: Jobs attracted people, these new people needed stores and services, thus generating new employment, and so on. But there were other reasons for the departure of the whites. Some simply didn't like the city, and, despite the early postwar wringing of hands over the sameness and psychoses of suburbia, did like detached houses and gardens. The federal government responded with generous mortgage guarantees that made it easier than ever before to buy a new house in the suburbs, as 5 million did under federal programs in postwar years. The government also cooperated by building highways to make commuting easier for those who still came in to the city to work.

The black man's problem was that he found it hard to follow the exodus, even in order to get a job. To get to the suburbs from where he lived required a long commute. Public transportation had been stretched to the breaking point by suburban growth and, where it did exist, was scheduled to bring commuters *into* the city during the morning rush hour, not take them out. The commute could also be expensive: The New York Traffic Commission has estimated that a Harlem worker spends $40 per month to get to factories on Long Island or in Westchester County, where many of the new employment centers are. Cars are expensive to buy and operate, and parking places hard to find on city streets.

The black man found it harder still to buy a suburban house. He was kept out, in part, by blunt and implacable racism. Most surburban realtors would not show him a house, much less sell him one, and builders and mortgage bankers also cooperated in the system. So did the federal government. The Federal Housing Administration, in the postwar years, warned in one of its underwriting manuals that "if a neighborhood is to retain stability, it is necessary that properties shall continue to be occupied by the same social and racial group." Similar warnings against suburban integration were part of FHA's standard forms until 1967.

He was also kept out by economics, given the tragic correlation between class and race. There was a process of natural

selection at work: The newest and most desirable houses were in the suburbs; they cost more to buy or rent; and so the suburbs became enclaves of the middle and upper classes. The poor got what the suburbanites left behind.

The selection was not entirely natural. As each new development was built on the outer edge of metropolis, it became first a self-styled community, then a town, township, borough, or municipality with its own home guard of officials and employees. Each of these mini-governments had at least two effective weapons to keep anyone from building housing that would make their exclusive communities less exclusive.

Curiously, both of the weapons were designed with high purposes in mind. The first, zoning, was intended to bring about more rational uses of land and more pleasing patterns of development. But the suburbs found in it an excellent means for maintaining class purity: Who among the poor could afford two-acre lots? The second defensive weapon, somewhat more technical, was the government's requirement that a "workable program for community improvement" be adopted by any municipality intending to construct housing using the major federal aids. The purpose of the requirement was to ensure that, before they got federal money, local governments were doing their jobs in such areas as code enforcement and relocation of families displaced by public landtaking. Ironically, it was used by the suburbs as a convenient veto over federally aided housing, which nearly all housing for the poor must be: They could simply refuse or fail to adopt a "workable program."

Metropolis is a web of these small jurisdictions, crisscrossed by countless special districts, and the city is at the center of the web. For the blacks, the jurisdictional strands often seem to be made of barbed wire.

The Making of the Slum-ghettos

The result of postwar patterns of growth, by the mid-1960's, was that more than half of the nation's blacks lived in the cities (and less than 8 per cent in the suburbs). They ac-

counted for more than a quarter of the total population in the big cities within metropolitan areas of a million or more. They were a majority in Washington, Newark, and Gary. Washington's black population, in fact, has passed the two-thirds point —while the black percentage of the population in the entire Washington metropolitan area remained virtually constant.

The white exodus had taken on the aspect of flight. The National Advisory Commission on Civil Disorders constructed an index of white "outflow" from the cities by comparing change in their white populations to growth in the nation's white population as a whole. In the 1950's, by its measure, the outflow—the differential between the decline in the cities' white populations and what should have been their share of over-all growth—was 5.8 million. In the years 1960–66 alone, the outflow was 5 million. The annual rate of whites actually leaving the cities in that period, by Census Bureau count, was 140,000 per year. Since 1966, it has increased to 500,000 per year.

The pattern of black-white separation is repeated within the cities themselves. Sociologists Karl and Alma Taeuber several years ago worked out an index of urban segregation that indicates the percentage of blacks that would have to move from one part of the city to another to achieve a statistically perfect racial distribution.[3] They applied the index to 207 cities and found that the average was 86—that is, 86 per cent of the Negroes would have to move out of the blocks they lived in if complete proportional distribution, block by block, were to be achieved. The Taeubers found that the index had not changed much since 1940, but a recent Census Bureau study indicated that, in many cities, segregation is on the increase. The bureau counted the number of Negroes living in census tracts with 75 per cent or more Negro residents in 1960 and 1965. In all but one of twelve selected cities, the number of Negroes living in these predominantly black areas increased over the five-year period. In Cleveland, for example, it went from 72 to 80 per

cent of the Negro population; in Shreveport, from 79 to 90 per cent.

The great black ghettos stretch for miles in the largest cities, and they are growing in both population and area. Real Estate Research Corporation, an economic consulting firm, conducts field surveys of racial change in Chicago neighborhoods; in 1967, found that 2.9 blocks per week were shifting from white to black, mainly those on the ghettos' edges. In 1968, the rate rose to 5.1 blocks per week.

Migration, however, is no longer the factor it once was in the ghettos' growth. Southern farm employment, according to the Department of Agriculture, has just about found its minimum level. Nor do very many any longer think of the big cities as the promised land. Inmigration of blacks to the cities all but stopped in the years 1966–68, according to the Census Bureau. Still, the ghettos now contain within themselves the major means of their continuing growth: 100,000 blacks were added to the cities' populations in those two years through natural increase, the excess of births over deaths. Since 1950, nearly 80 per cent of all Negro births have been in the cities (and 76 per cent of white births have been in the suburbs). Fertility rates among Negro women are half again as high as among whites, and the Negro population is, in the aggregate, younger.

The significance of all this is more than statistical. "Our nation is moving towards two societies, one black, one white— separate and unequal," read the famous warning of the Commission on Civil Disorders. By the middle of this decade, metropolis already was there.

The Way It Is

The commission devoted much of its report to a documentation of inequality. This was, in outline, the picture that it drew of life in the spreading slums and ghettos:

The housing is the worst in the city. How bad is hard to say without inspection; the statistics can be misleading. In

1960, for example, the official national figures for fourteen cities showed an average of 38 per cent of their nonwhite residents to be living in substandard dwellings (deteriorated, dilapidated, or lacking full plumbing). At the same time, however, an independent survey in Newark showed 91 per cent of all dwelling units in one ghetto area to be substandard. Similarly, national figures for ten metropolitan areas showed 22 per cent of the housing occupied by nonwhites to be overcrowded, as against 8 per cent of that occupied by whites. But how accurate can any measurement of overcrowding be when the people inside are afraid to admit it for fear of eviction? What is certain is that slum housing costs more than it should: Nonwhites in the same ten areas were paying 35 per cent of their incomes for rent. Part of this is a "color tax": In selected Chicago census tracts, whites and Negroes were paying the same rents, but the whites' housing was larger, less crowded, and in better condition than that of the Negroes. More than 30 per cent of the Negro units in the Chicago tracts were deteriorated or dilapidated; only 11 per cent of the white units were.

At midday, the streets are filled with idle men, particularly young men. There were, in 1967, 318,000 unemployed in the slums (including 98,000 teenagers), but that is only part of the problem: Another 716,000 were *under*employed; that is, either out of the labor force altogether, working part time but wanting to work full time, or working full time and earning less than a poverty-level income. The lower the income, the less likely it is that these men in the street will live with their families; in 1966, 42 per cent of all Negro families earning less than $3,000 a year were headed by a female, and the number is rising in the slums. Illegitimate births also are on the rise; in many slums the rate exceeds 50 per cent. On every index of social distress— juvenile delinquency, venereal disease, families on welfare —the slum scores depressingly higher than the rest of the city.

There is fear in the faces. The probability of Negro slum residents suffering from crime (excepting larceny) is 78 per cent higher than for whites in the metropolitan area. A Negro woman is 3.7 times more likely than a white woman to be raped. Slum residents complain about police brutality, but they complain more about the lack of law enforcement.

The children play in these streets. Three times as many Negro children as white drop out of school before the ages sixteen to seventeen. Those that stay fall further behind national achievement averages in verbal and reading ability with each year in school; by the twelfth grade, they are 3.3 grades behind in their test scores. The chances are nearly eight in ten that the city child attends a school that is, in fact if not by law, segregated. By everyone concerned with the educational system—administrators, teachers, parents, students—black schools are considered inferior, and live up to it. Teachers have less experience and lower qualifications than in other schools; the buildings are more crowded, and older. In Detroit, thirty schools dedicated during the administration of President U. S. Grant are still in use in the slums.

This endless litany of despair is what defines a slum: It is a place of blight and degradation, and, like the poor, has always been with us. But the slums of the cities are also ghettos, bringing poverty and racial confinement into deadly coalescence. What this can do to the human spirit has to be experienced to be truly known. The impact is described this way by psychologist Kenneth Clark, who spent forty years of his life in Harlem:

> Human beings who are forced to live under ghetto conditions and whose daily experience tells them that almost nowhere in society are they respected and granted the ordinary dignity and courtesy accorded to others will, as a matter of course, begin to doubt their own worth. Since every human being depends upon his cumulative experiences with others for clues as to how he

should view and value himself, children who are consistently
rejected understandably begin to question and doubt whether
they, their family, and their group really deserve no more respect from the larger society than they receive.[4]

In the matter of employment, for example, "Negroes often
dread to try for jobs where Negroes have never worked before," Dr. Clark has said. "The Negro youth is caught in a
vicious cycle: Poor preparation means poor jobs and low
socio-economic status. Low status and poor jobs result in poor
preparation for the next generation to come."

And again: "Not only is the pathology of the ghetto self-
perpetuating but one kind of pathology breeds another. The
child born in the ghetto is more likely to come into a world of
broken homes and illegitimacy; and this family and social instability is conducive to delinquency, drug addiction, and
criminal violence." These are, said Dr. Clark, "symptoms of
the contagious sickness of the community"—a sickness passed
on from generation to generation, a contagion to which many
immigrants to the urban slum-ghetto quickly fall victim.

The destructive cycles of which Dr. Clark writes have been
in motion through the twentieth century and have intensified
with each wave of Negro migration to the cities. Such cycles
are responsible for the existence of an "underclass" in the
slums and ghettos. Members of this underclass are not especially pleasant people to be around, a fact that must be faced
and that adds still another cyclical turn: Whites look at these
socially objectionable characteristics and ascribe them to race
rather than the enforced cruelties of the ghetto environment.
The looks in the eyes of whites, mirrors of identity for the
black child, harden—and so it goes.

These cycles also do much to explain why the underclass is
joined at the barricades by blacks with jobs and education.
Negroes who take the first few painful steps up the ladder
most often find that the rungs just above have been removed.
They can get so far and no further into the white society; a
Negro with a college education can look forward to a lifetime

income less than that of a white high school graduate, by current Commerce Department figures.

"Relative deprivation"—the term used by the Commission on Civil Disorders—can be as explosive as real deprivation. Says sociologist Lee Rainwater:

> The fact that even a significant minority of [riot] participants are members of seemingly stable families earning above poverty-level incomes tells us something about what is involved in exclusion from ordinary American society in a city as prosperous as Detroit or Los Angeles. . . . It is quite clear that people with incomes as high as $5,000 a year are really not able to feel that they participate in the broad spectrum of average American affluence and satisfaction. A community in which the great majority of the families must exist on significantly less than the median family income for the nation is a community of failures.[5]

The ghetto dweller is trapped in this community, pinned down by poverty and prejudice, and he feels it. A sense of confinement pervades its streets, intensifying every manifestation of social distress. Worse yet, he feels powerless to change the circumstances that surround him. Someone else owns the places where he works and shops; someone else runs the city. Someone else puts the limits on his life, and that someone is white.

The view of the white power structure from the ghetto is not a pleasant one. The Civil Rights Commission describes it this way:

> For many ghetto residents, the symbol of white authority is the policeman, who, as they see it, has often not provided protection for citizens within the ghetto, does not treat them with dignity and respect, and sees his role as that of keeping Negroes "in line" on behalf of the white community. In the view of ghetto residents the attitude of local government is exemplified by the inadequacy of sanitation services, and by the absence of needed health and recreational facilities and the transportation services that would make them accessible. The symbols of the

white business community are the merchant who sells inferior merchandise or who exploits the economic dependence
of Negroes by providing credit at exorbitant rates, and the
absentee landlord who reduces services and allows property
to deteriorate once Negroes become tenants.[6]

In the ghetto, over the years, these daily rejections by whites
have taken on symbolic significance. Every official slight becomes further evidence of racial prejudice. It doesn't take
much, in this kind of atmosphere, to start trouble. "The
ghetto residents who rebel have been angry for many years
about many things," sociologist Herbert Gans said in testimony before the Civil Disorders Commission. "And one day,
through a combination of circumstances, their anger boils
over into an incident, and more and more often now, the incident leads to a larger rebellion."

The Era of Civil Disorders

Before 1969 ends, the pattern of urban conflict may have
changed. There are, as will be seen, some indications that it is
changing already. But it remains important to understand the
what and why of the civil disorders of 1963–68—a period
when the nation still had time.

Those disorders contained an element of irrationality that
has defied exact analysis. They were like a ritual that only the
participants fully understood. To know the full depths of their
causes, it would have been necessary to photograph, while the
disorders were in progress, the mind of a teenager, exhilarated
to the point of near hysteria, as he threw the first rock through
the large plate glass window of a store; of a middle-aged
mother as she carefully but heavily picked her way through
the glass with an armful of small appliances; of an older man
who stood on the corner shouting obscenities at all within ear-
shot, black youths and white police alike.

What is known, from the accumulating reports of post-riot
investigations, is that there was a marked pattern to where the
disorders struck; how they started; what happened, and did

not happen, before they ran their course; and who participated. We are also learning, at least in general terms, what
the participants were trying to tell us.

The single most dramatic fact about the disorders to date
was their circumspection. They were, first of all, geographically
circumscribed to the slums and ghettos of the city. In nearly
every case, there were rumors of bands of Negroes heading for
white neighborhoods (or, in Los Angeles, cruising out on the
freeways) but these rumors proved false. Instead, riot activity
was concentrated where the blacks were concentrated.

In particular, it was concentrated on the shopping streets,
where, into the late hours of hot summer nights, the sidewalks are jammed with people. The charts of riots look like
black shoppers' maps of the city. Some residences did burn,
but generally as a result of fires that started in the stores and
spread. The burning was selective, but not entirely so: Many
of the hulks of buildings left by disorders had the word "soul"
on the remaining fragments of their windows.

These were not "race riots." Except for scattered incidents,
the only violent black-white confrontation was that between
riot participants and police. The Detroit disorders of 1967, in
fact, were partially integrated: 12 per cent of those arrested for
looting were white.

The violent activities of the participants have been largely
limited to looting and arson. There have been only sporadic
assaults and little shooting—by the rioters. The riots of 1967,
according to the Civil Disorders Commission, "involved
Negroes acting against local symbols of white American society—authority and property—rather than against white persons." The commission had this to say about gunfire in the
1967 riots:

> Of 23 cities surveyed by the commission, there had been reports
> of sniping in at least 15. What is probable, although the evi-
> dence is fragmentary, is that there was at least some sniping.
> What is certain is that the amount of sniping attributed to riot-
> ers—by law enforcement officials as well as the press—was highly

exaggerated. According to the best information available to the commission, most reported sniping incidents were demonstrated to be gunfire by either police or National Guardsmen.

Chilling confirmation is found in the report of the New Jersey State Select Commission on Civil Disorders, which dealt with the 1967 riots in Newark and elsewhere in the state. Twenty-six people died during Newark's three days and nights of horror, and twenty-four were black. Said the commission, "The location of death, the number of wounds, the manner in which the wounds were inflicted all raise grave doubts about the circumstances under which many of these people died."[7] The head of Newark's anti-poverty agency testified that charges of widespread sniping were used "as justification to shoot the people and homes." On the Sunday morning after the violence ended, state police systematically went through shopping streets shooting into undamaged stores with signs saying "soul" on their windows, the New Jersey commission reported.

Nearly every summer disorder has had its "triggering incident." The spring, 1968, riots following Martin Luther King's death have been the only ones that could be causally linked to a single national event. In half of the twenty-four disorders of 1967 investigated by the national commission, the triggering incident involved the police. In five of the cities, a protest demonstration triggered disorder; the protest in each case was directed at police.

Often the incident was trivial. Brandeis University's Lemberg Center for the Study of Violence has shown a direct relationship between the level of Negro grievances in a given community and the seriousness of the incident required to start disorder. But in no case was the incident an isolated one. The Civil Disorders Commission found that

> violence was generated by an increasingly disturbed social atmosphere in which typically not one, but a series of incidents occurred over a period of weeks or months prior to the outbreak

of disorder. . . . These earlier or prior incidents were linked in the minds of many Negroes to the pre-existing reservoir of underlying grievances. With each such incident, frustration and tension grew until at some point a final incident, often similar to those preceding it, occurred and was followed almost immediately by violence.

None of the investigators have concluded that the violence followed a plan. The President specifically directed the Civil Disorders Commission to look into the extent to which the 1967 disorders were or were not organized, and he gave it full access to FBI and other government files. "On the basis of all the information collected," its report stated, "the commission concludes that the urban disorders of the summer of 1967 were not caused by, nor were the consequence of, any organized plan or 'conspiracy.' Specifically, the commission has found no evidence that all or any of the disorders or the incidents that led to them were planned or directed by any organization or group—international, national, or local."

It is difficult, even dangerous, to ascribe specific purpose to the riots. The analyst cannot in one breath dismiss plan or organization as a major causative factor and, in the next, present a detailed list of what the rioters want. There is, once again, this strain of irrationality to the disorders. Sociologist Nathan Glazer, in the British journal *Encounter,* called them "spontaneous rebellions, carried out impulsively by people who are, in a word, fed up with American white society." Another sociologist, in an unpublished analysis, says those who have protested in the ghetto have done so "as involuntarily as one screams in pain. [It is] a near-uncontrollable response." Nor, as the Civil Disorders Commission pointed out, were all rioters rebels with a cause: Some "may not have shared either the conditions or the grievances of their Negro neighbors; some may have cooly and deliberately exploited the chaos created out of frustration by others; some may have been drawn into the melee merely because they identified with, or wished to emulate, others."

Yet the number and nature of participants in the riots makes clear that the disorders were communal acts carried out by people in neighborhoods that had a great many grievances against society. On behalf of the Civil Disorders Commission, the University of Michigan's Institute for Social Research, in early 1968, interviewed 5,700 blacks and whites in fifteen cities on the subject of the disorders.[8] Most of the blacks avoided the word "riot" in describing the disorders; they also avoided the words "revolt" and "rebellion." The word they used again and again, the survey report said, was "protest." As such, the respondents found the disorders "partly or wholly justified" and "more likely . . . helpful to the Negro cause than hurtful."

The Civil Disorders Commission drew the following "profile of a rioter"; it says a great deal about the nature of the protest:

> The typical rioter in the summer of 1967 was a Negro unmarried male between the ages of 15 and 24. He was in many ways very different from the stereotype. He was not a migrant. He was born in the state and was a lifelong resident of the city in which the riot took place. Economically his position was about the same as his Negro neighbors who did not actively participate in the riot.
>
> Although he had not, usually, graduated from high school, he was somewhat better educated than the average inner-city Negro, having at least attended high school for a time. Nevertheless, he was more likely to be working in a menial or low-status job as an unskilled laborer. If he was employed, he was not working full time and his employment was frequently interrupted by periods of unemployment. He feels strongly that he deserves a better job and that he is barred from achieving it, not because of lack of training, ability, or ambition, but because of discrimination by employers.
>
> He rejects the white bigot's stereotype of the Negro as ignorant and shiftless. He takes great pride in his race and believes that in some respects Negroes are superior to whites. He is hostile to whites, but his hostility is more apt to be a product

of social and economic class than of race; he is almost equally hostile toward middle-class Negroes.

He is substantially better informed about politics than Negroes who were not involved in the riots. He is more likely to be actively engaged in civil rights efforts, but is extremely distrustful of the political system and of political leaders.

In short, he is alienated, he is impatient, and he is warning us that he can no longer tolerate the conditions of life in the slums and ghettos.

3

Damaged

In

Delivery

In fairness to the proprietors of the Great Society, it must be said that the business of changing people's lives is not an easy one. Government, in this country, simply has not been geared to do it. Federal institutions wage war and shoot rockets with a marvelous efficiency but turn bumbling on the city streets; local governments have been largely public housekeepers and are poorly suited to more demanding human tasks.

There is, says the businessman and Civil Disorders Commission aide Victor Palmieri, "a steadily widening gap between accepted public purposes of goals and the operational capabilities of public agencies. It is one thing to certify a few city blocks for demolition and rebuilding. It is quite another to merge physical and human renewal—through specialized education, job training, health services, counseling, recreation—and to attempt to regenerate not simply a place, but a community."[1]

Palmieri may exaggerate the degree to which slum-ghetto improvement has become an "accepted public purpose," but his basic diagnosis is discouragingly accurate: "Our new aspirations carry with them a demand for competence—for institutional copesmanship, if you will—that is greater in orders of magnitude than we now command."

The inability—or unwillingness—to cope extends from top to bottom of the process by which national urban policy is carried to the point of delivery. The executive branch of the federal government splits urban tasks among separate departments and agencies, each with its own jealously guarded piece of the action. The most urban—HUD, HEW, Transportation, Office of Economic Opportunity (OEO)—are also the newest arms of the federal establishment, lacking entrenched internal and external constituencies to help them when budget battles are fought.

They also lack competitively strong ties to Congress. Congress, it is claimed, is the body most directly representative of the public will, but Congress has institutionalized two biases which give an anti-urban warp to its workings: Rural representatives continue to exercise disproportionate power, despite reapportionment; and southern representatives, because of their political longevity, largely run the show. This latter fact gives racial considerations a large and negative weight when urban programs come up for discussion.

Those that survive pass into the hands of a federal bureaucracy that has grown to the point of unmanageability, particularly in its regional outposts beyond the capital. The way it operates was studied in detail by an interagency task force of federal regional officials, which, in 1968, examined the handling of federal urban programs in Oakland, California. The task force found that some of the regional offices Oakland had to work with covered as many as eleven states (HUD) and some took in only a part of California (the Commerce Department); some could approve applications and some had to pass them on to Washington; some had streamlined application processes (five steps to an Economic Development Administration loan) and some had not (130 steps, requiring an average of 3,729 days, for an urban renewal project).[2] Every agency had its own way of doing business, to the point of applying varying requirements for citizen participation that resulted in rival citizen boards warring within the city.

Oakland's own government did not come off totally unscathed. The task force found little agreement "as to the order of importance of the many problems facing Oakland or the order in which they should be given priority." The Civil Disorders Commission, reviewing the operations of local governments in general, concurred. In its report, it said that local governments exhibit "little or no meaningful coordination" among their agencies and about the same degree of willingness to communicate with their disadvantaged citizens. From the ghetto, the commission said, "city government appears distant and unconcerned, the possibility of effective change remote."

The result of all this is that many of the programs aimed at the slum-ghettos—in housing, in poverty, in education— have built into them, at some point in the process between conception and effectuation, the seeds of their own frustration. Many others, emerging from Washington more or less intact, are hampered by their handling in "the field." And some, when put into operation, merely serve to uncover far more problems than they could hope to solve.

A classic case is the federal urban renewal program, whose nearly twenty-year history involves all three of these circumstances. The program was enacted in 1949 as part of the first major postwar expansion of the housing and slum-clearance efforts of the New Deal. Basically, it provided for acquisition of blighted properties by cities through the power of eminent domain, then sale of the properties to private developers or public agencies for "redevelopment" according to an approved plan. The federal government would pay a large share—at first two-thirds, later 80 per cent—of the "project cost," defined as the difference between the cost of acquiring the land and the price paid by the redevelopers, plus the cost of clearing the land and installing necessary improvements such as streets and sewers. Before the land could be cleared, the city had to find "decent, safe, and sanitary" housing for those who would be displaced, the first time a requirement this generous to the victims of progress had appeared in federal law.

Urban renewal began with nearly as many goals as it had

supporters. It offered, to begin with, the opportunity to "up-grade" the use of valuable urban land and, thus, to increase the city's tax base. It promised to create bright new urban environments that could compete with the suburbs for the affections of the middle class. It was a locally controlled program, yet it brought forth both federal and private money in large amounts. Finally, and uppermost in the minds of many, it would get rid of slums and replace them with sound new housing.

It soon became clear that, in operation, these goals tended to conflict. The city's desire to improve its tax situation sometimes led to choices of sites that, though scarcely slums at all, offered prime possibilities for new revenues. Private developers found few windfalls in renewal and had to be lured in: This meant offering attractive sites for profitable kinds of development, which housing for the poor definitely is not. Gradually, the original housing emphasis of the program yielded as "liberalizing" amendments were enacted authorizing use of renewal to build stores, office buildings, and institutions.

Washington found, after some bitter early experiences, that it could not leave the matter of relocating the displaced entirely to local control. Cities often paid only as much attention to relocation as they were forced to. As the years went on, urban renewal came under increasing attack from social critics for its handling of the slum dwellers.

In 1964, a young Columbia University faculty member named Martin Anderson (four years later an urban affairs adviser to Richard Nixon) published a book entitled *The Federal Bulldozer* urging outright repeal of urban renewal.[3] The book was largely an attack from the far right, but it contained an analysis of the federal government's own statistics that seemed to confirm the social critics' worst fears: In the first twelve years of the program, 126,000 dwelling units had been demolished for urban renewal, most inhabited by the poor; only 28,000 dwelling units had been built, very few for the poor. The government countered with a Census Bureau study indicating that at least 80 per cent of those displaced by urban renewal had moved to decent housing, but the damage had been done. The image of the federal bulldozer was lodged in the public mind: Urban renewal was the program that kicked poor people out of their homes and put up high-rise luxury apartments in their place.

The facts are more complicated—and more instructive of how federal programs can go wrong. The trouble with urban renewal is not what it is, but what it is not. Urban renewal, in the first place, is not a program for the over-all improvement of people's lives as well as their dwelling places. It was conceived as an instrument of physical development, a way of putting land under bricks and mortar. The real failure of relocation is related to this fact: Urban renewal uprooted the people least able to cope with that kind of disruption. It changed their lives, but it did not possess the means of helping them deal with change. All that could be done under urban renewal laws was to help them find new places to live and pay part of their moving expenses. If, in the process, neighborhood ties were broken, jobs lost, fragile family relationships shattered, there was nothing urban renewal could do. The city could help on its own, but few cities did.

The poor paid heavily for other people's progress, and it took the government sixteen years to realize that there were more significant goals to urban improvement than physical goals. The Model Cities program, enacted in 1966, is what urban renewal should have been if the objective was not just to clear slums but to improve the lives of slum dwellers. It provides the means of concentrating on slum neighborhoods all available resources—federal and local, public and private— and all available tools, from urban renewal to employment, health, welfare, and education programs. It has some problems of its own, but that is another story.

The second thing urban renewal is not, surprisingly, is a housing program for the poor. Urban renewal is a tool, and a powerful one, to make land and money available for development. That development, by recent obligation, must include low-income housing—but the housing is built under other programs, not urban renewal. Many of the failings of urban renewal are directly related to the nearly total failure of other federal programs to provide low-income housing in more than token quantities.

Chief among these programs is public housing, enacted during the New Deal and expanded, at least in intent, by the same 1949 act that created urban renewal. This was the act stating the sweeping, and subsequently embarrassing, national goal of a "decent home and suitable living environment for every American family." Among its provisions was the authorization of 810,000 units of public housing over the next six years. Only in 1968, nineteen years later, could the government claim to have built that number of units of public housing—not since 1949, but over the entire history of the program.

Why did the nation default on its 1949 pledge? One reason is that public housing has been fought tooth and nail by an alliance of conservatives and special interests in the housing, real estate, and mortgage-finance fields. Neither the realtors nor the housing "industry"—a chaotic nonsystem composed of small entrepreneurs and characterized by restrictive labor practices, capricious financing, and nineteenth-century technology—have ever given the poor a product they could afford. Many builders willingly admit that it is impossible to break even on low-income housing without some form of subsidy. Yet they and the realtors fought hard to keep government from entering a market they would not, and probably could not, serve.

That is not the whole story, however. In many fiscal years, fewer public housing units are built than have been authorized by Congress. The fundamental reason for the dismal production record in public housing is that no one wants to live next door to it. Often it is not an attractive neighbor. Congress has placed such stringent limits on costs and amenities that it takes heroic effort by designers and administrators to make public housing anything but a bleakly negative blot on the skyline. By its nature, moreover, public housing concentrates the poor and their problems: Once families begin to progress and make a decent income, they must, by law, be evicted. The increasing correlation of urban poverty and color has added the factor of racial concentration as well. In most cities, each public-housing tower is its own self-contained, high-rise ghetto.

The failure of public housing is well known. It is roundly disliked by everyone but the poor, who, in most cities, have their names on waiting lists by the tens of thousands—more than 150,000 in New York City alone. Less publicity has been given the failure of another program, rent supplements, which started life in 1965 as perhaps the most promising new housing tool since the New Deal.

Rent supplements were introduced as an appendage to generous federal mortgage guarantees, also relatively new, allowing private or nonprofit sponsors to build housing for moderate-income families with minimum cash outlays (the so-called Section 221d3 program.) The rent supplement program brings this housing within reach of the poor: Families who cannot meet the rental schedule and who fall into specified categories of need, including all those who live in blighted dwellings, pay one-quarter of their monthly income and the government pays the rest. If their incomes rise, the families are not evicted. Instead, the share of the rent paid by the government—the "supplement"—simply decreases. The program, said President Johnson when he introduced it to Congress, "will permit us to encourage housing in which families of different incomes . . . can live together."

The President did not mention families of different races living together, but Congress got the message anyway and the knives came out. Despite support of groups ranging from the American Bankers Association to the National Farmers Union, the program squeaked through the House by six votes and the Senate by seven. Appropriations to run the program in 1966 passed the Senate by a single vote. Appropriations for fiscal 1967 passed the House by four. Representative Paul Fino, Republican defender of the Bronx, said at one point during the debate: "This program does not deserve so much as a plugged nickel. . . . The planners down at HUD hope to use subsidized lower-middle-income tenants to blockbust certain neighborhoods in our big cities and suburbs."

The program that came out of Congress was significantly different from the one which the President sent in. Congress added a rider giving local communities a virtual veto over use of rent supplements even in privately sponsored housing. It also applied tight limitations on "amenities"—even four-bedroom units, for example, could have only a single bathroom—which, when combined with FHA's formula fixing construction cost limits according to rental expectations, has meant that the quality of rent-supplement housing is likely to be even lower than that of public housing.

The inevitable result is that rent supplements do little to lessen the concentration of the poor. When a family's income rises, it looks for something better rather than staying put. Rent-supplement housing shares the stigma of public housing; it therefore shares the built-in limitations on the degree that it can improve the environment of the poor. There are few places it can be built without raising neighborhood ire.

Another set of limitations, contradictions, and perversions plague federal programs designed to lift slum-ghetto residents out of poverty. Here the classic tragedy is the welfare system, which the Civil Disorders Commission called "a labyrinth of federal, state, and local legislation" and which, in 1968, doled out $8.8 billion, just over half in federal money. The way it is doled out, in the commission's words, "contributes materially to the tensions and social disorganization that have led to civil disorders" and alienates "the taxpayers who support welfare, the social workers who administer it, and the poor who depend on it." Daniel Patrick Moynihan, White House adviser on urban affairs, believes that "the probability is strong that the present welfare system is serving to maintain the poorest groups in society in a position of impotent fury."

Not all of the faults in welfare are federal. It is at the state level that the "man-in-the-house" rule (deemed unconstitutional by the Supreme Court) has required fathers to choose between leaving their families or seeing them go hungry. It is the states which have imposed residency requirements (also now banned by the Court) which have meant, as the Civil Disorders Commission pointed out, that "those in greatest need—desperately poor families arriving in a strange city—are prevented from receiving the boost that might give them a fresh start." And it is the states and cities that often make social workers into the wardens of the ghetto, second only to the police as objects of fear and hatred.

Until recently, the federal government's role in creating the welfare mess has been mainly the result of calculated neglect. In 1967, federal assistance reached about 8 million people a month. Of these, 2.8 million were elderly or handicapped, whose numbers are decreasing; 3.9 million were children of poor families, whose numbers are greatly increasing; and 1.3 million were the parents of these children (more than 1 million, their mothers). These seem like large numbers, but they represent only a third of those who need assistance. The federal government has chosen to regard poverty as primarily a state and local problem, and the states and localities have not been uniformly generous. In New York State, the Aid for Dependent Children (AFDC) program provides $244 a month for a family of four. In Mississippi, the same family would get $35 a month.

Federal laws, however, have made a direct contribution to the dependency of the welfare recipient by requiring that anything he makes be deducted from his assistance payments, dollar for dollar. And, in 1967, Congress passed a pair of welfare amendments that could, if they strictly followed their sponsors' intent, have resulted in millions of the most needful mothers and children receiving no assistance at all. The first, repealed in 1969, would have frozen the percentage of children who can receive AFDC assistance in any state to the percentage receiving it in January, 1968. The second required all adult welfare recipients to take training or jobs, and provided new programs to increase training opportunities and child-care facilities. The Civil Disorders Commission warned, however, that if the get-out-and-work mandate were rigorously enforced against AFDC mothers, these programs would turn out to be vastly inadequate in size.

The "family-assistance system," unveiled by President Nixon in August, 1969 as a substitute for welfare, follows the direction of this second amendment. While couched in conservative rhetoric (the President trotted out his campaign phrase of "getting everyone able to work off welfare rolls and onto payrolls"), it strikes at several of welfare's most serious deficiencies, including the disadvantagement of the working poor. A family of four would receive a minimum of $1,600 from the federal government (hopefully to be supplemented by the states) and could keep the first $60 per month it earned plus 50 cents of each dollar earned thereafter.

Aside from the question of adequacy of assistance, the program is dependent, as was the second 1967 welfare amendment, on the supply of job and training opportunities and child-care facilities, which the President pledged to increase. To do so would require far more than the $4 billion that he said the new system would cost, most of which would go into the floor to be put under the incomes of the working poor. Without additional money, the prospect is that AFDC rolls will simply become family-assistance rolls. The tragedy is that many mothers on AFDC would like to work: A New York City survey of 1,500 welfare mothers indicated that 70 per cent (and 80 per cent of those who were Negro) would prefer jobs to staying home. But first they need a place to care for their children and then they need training and job opportunities.

So do their sons and husbands. The dearth of employment opportunities is "the master problem" of the slum-ghetto, Moynihan has said. Yet, until 1962, the federal government had no manpower program at all. Since then it has built up a bewildering variety of them, with a total budget of more than $2 billion for fiscal 1969, but without benefit of a guiding strategy. "The programs were piled one on top of another, without any real reference to each other," commented *Congressional Quarterly* in May, 1968. "The result was a duplication in some services and a situation in which many programs did not have enough funds to carry out their aims." *Congressional Quarterly* listed fifteen such programs at the time, lodged in the departments of Labor, Interior, and HEW, and in the Veterans Administration and OEO.

In early 1968, the Johnson Administration added another program designed to meet the special needs of the slum-ghetto unemployed, in this case by mustering private enterprise. The President asked Henry Ford II to form a National Alliance of Businessmen whose goal would be to hire and train, on the job, 500,000 "hard-core unemployed" in fifty cities. The "hard-core" were defined as: anyone who had an income below the poverty level and who was also a member of a minority group, a teenager, young adult, aging adult, or physically handicapped person of any age; or anyone with less than an eighth-grade education. The federal role in the program, known as JOBS (Job Opportunities in the Business Sector), was to help pay the companies for job training and for such addenda as literacy training, transportation, health services, and counseling.

Hiring began in May, 1968. By January, 1969, the National Alliance was able to report that 12,500 firms had placed 125,000 persons; of these, 85,000 were still on the job, which made for a highly respectable retention rate of 68 per cent. It was a sizable accomplishment, although a fifth of the placements were in a single company, General Motors, and, as some critics pointed out, two-thirds of the placements did not involve JOBS subsidies and thus were exempt from federal training standards. The program has been expanded to additional cities, with a 1969 goal of 200,000 placements—assuming continued prosperity.

The major accomplishment of the National Alliance may have been the introduction of 12,500 firms to urban unemployment problems and their victims, rather than the actual job placements. Even if the three-year goal of 500,000 is achieved, says manpower specialist Garth Magnum, "we will never notice the difference."

A more significant limitation is that JOBS will not create jobs. It will simply train people for jobs that already exist. In doing so, moreover, it could cause certain inequities. Faced with pledges to meet, and with the prospect of federal help, a company might choose to hire a dropout from the streets over a conscientious Negro high school graduate who has worked hard to earn his opportunity.

The View from the Street

The list of built-in deficiencies and inevitable frustrations in federal urban programs could be expanded indefinitely. In the end, it all comes down to the difference these programs make at the point of delivery, on the street. In some cases, it is at this point that a program changes from something that could help to something that harms. A lot depends on how it is delivered and by whom.

The face of government to the ghetto resident is not the smiling face of the mayor or a senator in a newspaper photograph: It is the hard face behind the window of an agency telling him what he can't have, or can't do. The face belongs to a clerk who is underpaid and overworked, who may be in government service for the security (or for lack of a better offer), and to whom this is just one more client with troubles he or she really can't solve. Involvement just means more papers to fill out and file.

Reform movements have tended to further depersonalize the face of government. The emphasis on neat administrative lines of authority has made of government agencies what one political scientist called "islands of functional power." Those who work in these islands are often more mindful of their colleagues' opinions—not just at the local level, but in counterpart agencies of federal and state government—than of the needs of other departments, or indeed, of the clients. Those who become expert in the bureaucracy are expert on programs and procedures, not necessarily on the problems of people, which often do not fit neatly into the pigeonholes of departmental responsibility.

Many of those who deliver the programs come from the white lower-middle class, where resentment of the blacks is most prevalent. Political and civil service jobs have been a traditional entry point for ethnic immigrants and their sons and daughters. "The Irish didn't go around shouting 'Irish Power!'" Whitney Young is fond of saying. "They just moved in and took over the police department." In many cities, they continue to hold on to it, and other ethnic groups have made similar strongholds of other branches of government. Blacks are grossly underrepresented in government jobs. Pressure to get them in breeds further resistance among the whites who have the jobs now.

All of this goes on in a period of growing awareness that the best of programs can do more harm than good if they are dispensed in an inefficient or insulting way at the street level. "We're in a time when it's less important *what* you do than *how* you do it," says Allan Talbot of the New York State Urban Development Corporation. And increasingly, the "how" includes letting the ghetto residents do much of it themselves.

The idea has had its ups and downs since first officially introduced in the War on Poverty as "maximum feasible participation" of the poor. The meaning of this ungainly phrase was that, to the greatest extent possible, the poor themselves would run OEO programs in their communities, thus building pride, competence, and power. Father Henry Browne, of New York's West Side, put it his own way before the Ribicoff Committee: "It is my conviction that 90 to 95 per cent of the poor people do not need the crutch-like services tendered by caseworkers, the 9-to-5 types, but education and organization and at times a bit of inspiration and even agitation."

That's what the poor got from OEO, to their lasting benefit. But agitation doesn't sit well with city hall. Many mayors resented federal money going to "troublemaking" groups in their cities, money entirely outside of their control. Repeated attempts were made to discredit the OEO community-action programs with charges of waste and radicalism, and, in 1967, Congress passed the Green Amendment giving the mayors substantial control over the operation of these programs. But the durability of the basic idea of community involvement was shown when, at the same time, HUD made citizen participation a requirement of the Model Cities program. "There must be some form of organizational structure, existing or newly established, which embodies neighborhood residents in the process of policy and program planning and program implementation and operation," say the HUD guidelines. The leadership "must consist of persons whom neighborhood residents accept as representing their interests."

There is no disputing that these guidelines slowed the early planning stages of the program and even engendered an epidemic of (nonviolent) conflict in applicant cities across the country. But a report issued by HUD on first-year planning in three of these cities—Atlanta, Seattle, and Dayton—indicates that it may have been very much worthwhile.[4] The report, the work of the consulting firm of Marshall Kaplan, Gans, and Kahn, points out that all three cities minimized citizen participation in the early stages of the planning process, were forced by community pressures and prodding from HUD to expand it, and eventually worked it out well enough to support the judgment that they produced "creditable plans" acceptable both to city hall and to the neighborhoods. More important, the report gives the distinct impression that civic business in the three cities may never be done again in quite the traditional exclusionary, closehanded ways. In Dayton, the citizens planning council of the Model Cities area already has been given a voice in the operation of other programs. The area had been the scene of three riots just before Model Cities came along. The program, concludes the report on the three cities, has given the residents at least some hope that government can be a vehicle for improvement of their lives.

This, along with other evidence growing out of recent urban history, supports the view that only when the poor are involved in the operation of programs do the programs work. When the poor are excluded, the programs, though designed for their benefit, breed resentment rather than hope. The Civil Disorders Commission concurs, citing a report, prepared by the University of Chicago, on the operations of an OEO community-action agency in a large midwestern city. "As much as the area residents are involved, listened to, and even heeded," the report said, "it becomes fairly clear that the relationship is still one of the superordinate-subordinate, rather than one of equals." The involvement of the residents, the report continued, came "only after programs [had] been written, after policies [had] already operated for a time or already been formulated, and, to a large degree, only in formal and infrequent meetings rather than in day-to-day operations." The city was Detroit, and the report was prepared just before Detroit exploded in the summer of 1967. The commission suggested that inadequate citizen participation in both Detroit and New Haven was one reason the large number of programs aimed at the ghettos in the two cities had failed to stave off violence.

Kenneth Simmons, a young black architect who was a consultant in the planning of an experimental neighborhood center in New York City, concluded that no new institution set up to help the ghetto would work unless residents were involved in every step of its creation. Even badly needed new schools are resented if they are simply plunked into the community from above. Simmons tells of standing at the construction site of one school in the South Bronx. Along the fence were ranged a group of idle young men from the neighborhood, and there was deep hostility on their faces: Every day they had watched the mainly white construction workers arrive in their big cars, do their day's labor, then leave for the suburbs. The young men were unemployed. When that school opens, said Simmons, there will be no rejoicing in the community—the community had no role in bringing it into being and, barring change between now and then, will have no say in its operation. Community involvement would make all the difference, would surround the completion of the school with all the joy and pride "of an old-fashioned barn-raising," said Simmons, who believes that's the way it has to be.

Community involvement complicates every step of the process: It would be much easier to rebuild the ghettos by fiat, as Baron Haussmann rebuilt Paris. And the complications are multiplied by the increasing escalation of demands by ghetto residents for self-determination. Helped along by the oratory of Black Power, the issue has gone beyond community involvement to community control.

The problems this raises for even a sympathetic administrator of ghetto programs can be paralyzing. There is, at the outset, the question of who represents the community. Washington is a case in point. The burned out shopping streets of Washington, more than a year after the April, 1968, disorders, look much as they did the day that violence ended. The city had the will to reconstruct them, to build something better than had been there before; it had the money; it was ready to turn as much responsibility as possible over to the people in the stricken neighborhoods. What delayed reconstruction was that a multiplicity of organizations, some created on an *ad hoc* basis just after the riots, claimed to speak for these people—claimed control. Their ideas of how the job should be done varied widely, and they were locked in bitter infighting.

At one point, a similar dispute between community leaders threatened to scuttle Robert Kennedy's vast public-private plan for the improvement of the Bedford-Stuyvesant ghetto in Brooklyn. The disputants met in the office of Mitchell Sviridoff, then head of New York City's newly created Human Resources Administration (HRA). "After three hours of screaming and shouting, I proposed mediation," says Sviridoff, for twenty years a union official. The two sides each proposed lists of possible mediators, then took turns rejecting the names on the other's list. Finally they agreed on a respected Negro attorney from Kansas City, Missouri, Samuel Jackson (now Assistant Secretary of HUD). For months he sat almost as a judge, mediating the issues that divided the community.

Sviridoff, now a vice-president of the Ford Foundation, makes an interesting comment on the Bedford-Stuyvesant experience: "While the dispute surfaced around the issue of fund jurisdiction, what they were really scrapping over was the scarcity of funds," he says. "If there were enough money for what Bedford-Stuyvesant really needs, every one of these able people would be fully occupied. There are no villains in the story. On both sides the disputants are people dedicated to the community but frustrated by the very limited possibilities."[5]

Community control, of course, only removes the frustration of powerlessness. As Sviridoff's comment indicates, it may raise other frustrations unless accompanied by sufficient resources to get the job of community improvement done. Community control over the schools, which has become the major immediate object of black leaders in many cities, was debated at a 1967 Civil Rights Commission conference on ghetto education. At the conference, David K. Cohen, of the Harvard-MIT Joint Center for Urban Studies, warned that decentralization of the school system could give ghetto parents "phony power": They would still not have the money "to eradicate the damage done to their children by the schools" and might turn on each other in despair.

A similar theme emerged at a conference called by the American Institute of Architects to encourage volunteer design and planning services in the ghettos. The root problem, contended Washington architect Tunney Lee, "is the redistribution of power to the local group. . . . The only way you are going to resolve the thing in Harlem is for Harlem to elect its government, which will set its own priorities." Without disagreeing, Jonathan Barnett, an architect on the New York Planning Commission staff, cautioned that power would not turn out to be a panacea. Even if Harlem were to have its own leaders and hire its own planners to decide what should be done, said Barnett, "the present state of being able to handle urban problems in this country is such that it isn't going to help. . . . You can transfer the power structure all over the map, but until you have addressed yourself to what you would do with the power after you would get it, you won't do any better than at present."

The resources that ghetto communities need to solve their problems are human as well as monetary. An insistence on community control to the degree that only blacks can be involved often limits the supply of human resources. This can mean that things don't get done, or, if done, not well. To stay in the field of architecture: Only 1 per cent of that profession is black, a reprehensible fact. Those few who are black seldom get the opportunity to develop the kind of sophisticated skills needed to deal with the painfully difficult problems of building in the ghetto, which usually involve trying to create a silk-purse environment on a sow's ear budget—it takes the best talent around, black or white. Similarly, an insistence that all teachers in ghetto schools be black does not ease the problem of teacher recruitment, which is one of the major factors that contribute to making ghetto schools what they are.

These cautions are raised not to argue against community involvement, because for all its difficulties maximum feasible participation of ghetto residents has been permanently installed as an essential element of ghetto improvement. Blacks won't have it any other way. They cannot—will not—keep faith any longer with a white government that rebuffs them, ignores them, does things *to* them rather than *with* them. The Civil Disorders Commission has issued a warning of the consequences of allowing their faith to be lost. Says the commission, "No democratic society can long endure the existence within its major urban centers of a substantial number of citizens who feel gravely aggrieved as a group, yet lack confidence in the government to rectify perceived injustice and in their ability to bring about needed change."

Participation, involvement, control over one's destiny— these were not inventions of social scientists or the Economic Opportunity Act of 1964. They are part of a wide and deep movement that extends beyond the ghetto, extends world-wide, encompassing students, union members, white ethnic groups. If these drives are most intense in the ghetto, it is be-cause the sense of alienation is deepest there. The blacks are saying the white society can't have it both ways—can't keep them in the ghetto and run it from outside. They are asking for a share in running their own institutions and pointing out, with deadly accuracy, that whites haven't done that good a job of running them in the past.

At present, the black demands are virtually stalemating ghetto programs in many cities. Resentful and uncompre-hending administrators and bureaucrats and angry blacks engage in endless confrontations. How it all will come out depends on two factors: The first is whether the white man-agers of society have the will to negotiate—to make the trade offs that will give the blacks a voice and still let things get built and decided and done. "The issue is no longer *whether* the community is to be involved, but *how* it will be involved," said Sviridoff in early 1969.

The sooner this is realized, and the sooner the how is worked out, the better. For the second factor is how long the blacks will have the patience to negotiate.

4

Black
Pride

There are probably few whites in the urban business who have not, at one time or another in the past year or so, wished they were black. There has grown a spirit among the blacks that can be something to see—a brotherhood, a tough and aggressive pride, a truly fierce determination to wrest from white society what it has not been willing to give. The editor of an urban affairs magazine returned from a trip to Newark in early 1969 deeply impressed with this spirit: "They act like they own the world," she said. "The difference between the blacks and the tired old people in city hall is appalling. It makes you think you should just step aside and let them run things."

But there is a less inspiring side to it, too. The same editor wound up alone in Newark's Central Ward after dark and had her purse stolen. As she herself acknowledged, she should not have been there without a black companion; and others who know the district said she was lucky to get away without injury—simply because she was white. Apart from the matter of violence, there is an edge to black-white contact these days, a reserve and lack of trust on the part of the blacks that wasn't there as recently as a year or two ago. There is an undercurrent, to state it bluntly, approaching racism.

It is now necessary, and should not be, for a white man to defend writing about black attitudes. The defense goes like this: The blacks are not sole owners of "the problem" in the cities. It is compounded of a variety of malfunctions in the American system that misshape the society in which I, and my children, also live. Racial injustice itself warps this society, harming us in a real, if indirect, way. Therefore I have a direct stake in correcting these malfunctions, and, since they are created by white-run institutions, a special opportunity and responsibility to do so. This requires understanding, and dealing with, all aspects of the urban situation, and one key aspect is the mood of the blacks.

There is a temptation, of course, to say that it is their business and theirs alone. This temptation can arise out of resentment—if that's the way they want it, let them solve it—or out of compassion, an understanding of the history behind black anger at all things white and of the depth of desire for self-determination. But it contains the implication that they *are* the problem, rather than its prime victims, and that, within themselves, they carry the means of its solution. They do not: The solution, as will be seen, requires adjustments in the priorities, institutions, and practices of the larger society, which are, again, the business of all of us to bring about.

The enormous recent changes in the mood and spirit of the blacks have been largely stimulated by the black power movement, if a bag wide enough to hold Malcolm X and the "new" Whitney Young can be called a movement. The ideology of black power has been more shouted than expounded; its expression has been mainly in angry or mystical terms. In 1967, however, Stokely Carmichael and political scientist Charles V. Hamilton wrote *Black Power*, a book that remains the best inside analysis to date.[1] The components of black power, say Carmichael and Hamilton, are black self-determination and black self-identity. Its goals are "full participation in the decision-making process affecting the lives of black people, and recognition of the virtues in themselves as black people."

The blacks in America, Carmichael and Hamilton maintain, are ruled as a colony. The institutional form of racism in America is colonialism. Black politicians are hand-picked and co-opted by the white colonial power structure, so that a gap grows between the black masses and these "captive leaders." Black neighborhoods are denied political strength by gerrymandering and by rigged electoral systems such as at-large voting. They are denied economic strength as well: "Exploiters come into the ghetto from outside, bleed it dry, and leave it economically dependent on the larger system." The residents, like any colonial subjects, are robbed of human dignity and self-respect. Instead, they learn self-hatred.

American society offers avenues of escape into the mainstream, but only if the black man is willing to "disassociate [himself] from the black race, its culture, community, and heritage"—to become, in effect, white. This adaptive process deprives the black community of potential skills and brain power. Those who pass through it are picked by whites as black leaders, yet "have no viable constituency for which they can speak or act."

Black people must redefine themselves, must "reclaim their history, their culture . . . create their own sense of community and togetherness." Black Americans must feel a common bond to each other and to their African brothers; they must reject the values of middle-class America, which is "the backbone of institutional racism."

Political structures and institutions must be modernized; the old forms must be made responsive or replaced. To achieve this goal, black people must become more politically active, must choose their own leaders. And they must close ranks, as other ethnic groups did to achieve political strength. Politically, black power means coming together to deal from strength rather than weakness. Ultimately, perhaps, meaningful gains will come only through coalitions of blacks and whites with similar goals, but only if the blacks are strong enough and unified enough to be full partners.

Although Carmichael and Hamilton do not, in this book, advocate black nationalism or separatism, they do deride the concept of integration. All that integration has meant, they maintain, is that a few blacks make it, but the black people "have not suffered as individuals but as a group; therefore, their liberation lies in group action." And, while color blindness *may* (their emphasis) be a sound ultimate goal, race today is an overwhelming fact of national life. They find "despicable" the idea that to have a decent house or education, blacks must move into a white neighborhood or school.

Similarly, Carmichael and Hamilton do not advocate violence, but they do deride the nonviolent approach to obtaining civil rights, an approach "black people cannot afford and white people do not deserve." Whites must be made to understand that "there can be no social order without social justice"; blacks "should and must fight back." If the ghettos explode, it is because the fuse was lit "by white racist indifference and unwillingness to act justly."

This is black power at its most polite: Carmichael on a platform, or on the street, is something else. Even when expressed in calm and intellectual terms, however, the black power ideology contains the seeds of both hope and fear, of further black frustration as well as further black progress.

The most positive aspect of the ideology, and its most positive contribution to date, is that it has generated new pride and new aspiration among black people, particularly young black people. As psychologist Kenneth Clark, among others, pointed out, perhaps the most damaging aspect of Negro life in America is the continual assault on self-esteem. "The black man of today is at one end of a psychological continuum which reaches back in time to his enslaved ancestors," Negro psychiatrists William H. Grier and Price M. Cobbs have written.[2] "The practice of slavery stopped over a hundred years ago, but the minds of our citizens have never been freed." The strong emphasis in black power on competence, on black identity, can be the foundation for this ultimate form of freedom. Already it has produced an extraordinary generation of leaders.

Nor is there any arguing with the strategy of black unity.

Carmichael and Hamilton are accurate in their description of the Negro's exclusion from the political process; nearly 12 per cent of the population, blacks hold just over a tenth of 1 per cent of elective offices in this citadel of representative democracy. The way to get political power is to take it, and the way for blacks to take it is to work as a bloc. That's the way the political system operates. Black political leaders must be able to deliver (or withhold) votes to make an impact on the system, which means they must have a unified black constituency.

But political unity is one thing and racism is another. Carmichael and Hamilton absolve themselves from racism by defining it solely in terms of "subjugation." Yet racism has more subtle and no less real definitions, as whites well know—they invented many of them. Basically, it means judging a person not as a person but by his race or color. Usually it means a negative judgment: I am white and therefore superior; he is black and therefore inferior. It can, and does, work the other way around: I am black and therefore noble; he is white and therefore racist, exploitative, brutal, responsible for centuries of oppression. The concept of common white guilt runs through the book and the movement.

Black Americans have a culture and heritage to be proud of—even survival should be a source of pride given the conditions of their lives from slavery to the urban ghetto—but this pride takes on a racist tinge when cultural achievements are held up as evidence of superiority, or history is adjusted to make all blacks heroes and all whites villains. Black American culture is to be cherished and maintained, but the maintenance of "cultural integrity" that Carmichael and Hamilton advocate in keeping black communities intact smacks of racial purification.

White does not have to be ugly for black to be beautiful. Racism is what has put the black American where he is—and racism is contagious. It can also turn all too easily into hate, as it has in some black oratory. Blacks have ample reason to be angry, very angry, at whites and their society, but the proponents of black power do Americans of all colors a disservice when, instead of turning anger into a positive force, they fan anger into hate. Hate is something America has too much of already.

The Carmichael-Hamilton book handles the topic of violence with care; yet, in abruptly dismissing nonviolence, it leaves only one effective alternative. Its assertion of the right to self-defense is made more ominous by its picture of American society as an unremitting assault on blacks. From this point to a call to arms is a single short step.

This call is a call to mass suicide. The civil disorders to date have had an effect on the white majority—not enough of an effect, but a noticeable one. Concern about the cities, about poverty, about the blacks has increased measurably in some segments of the population even as resistance has grown in others. But this does not mean that more disorders will bring more concern, much less that guerrilla warfare will bring capitulation. The disorders moved a segment of public opinion because they were so clearly spontaneous, so demonstrably without plan, so poignantly linked to the less-than-human conditions of slum-ghetto life. Planned, tactical riots would be, at best, self-defeating.

At worst, they could lead to genocide. There is a great deal of talk in the streets about revolution, but instances of 12 per cent of any nation's population successfully carrying out a revolution are not to be found in history. The black revolutionaries might pick up allies—from among radical white students, for example—but, on the other hand, there is no reason to believe that they could count on anything like the entire black population, the 12 per cent, for support.

Carmichael and Hamilton treat the matter of black separatism with similar indirection, keeping their long-range options open for coalition with whites but rejecting racial integration with a fierceness that leaves separation the only alternative. The movement has since gone even farther in this direction. The impact of racial separation on the larger society will be dealt with in a subsequent chapter: The point to be made here is that it is a dead end for blacks if it becomes the end instead of the means. Never in American history has separate come out anything but unequal. "I feel that separatism we have had all the time," said Charles Evers, the Mississippi black leader, in a television interview. "That is nothing but a piece of corn bread for breakfast and some buttermilk for supper. All I had was separatism and I don't want that any more."

Black power has gotten involved in a geographical hang-up that could bring bitter frustration to black pride. The separatists are asking blacks to trade choice for power: to stay in the ghetto, do business there, vote there for the sake of cohesion, to give up hope of opening other options. In return they promise the satisfaction and rewards of self-determination. Yet they cannot deliver on this promise without the political and economic cooperation of the larger society, which inevitably will exact in return a measure of control over the deployment of money and power. Total self-determination thus becomes an illusion—not worth exchange of the hope of entering the larger society, where the big rewards are.

The tragedy is that the choice is unnecessary. Unity does not require that all blacks live in the same place. Earlier ethnic groups did not make it by staying in the slums. They stayed together politically, economically, helping each other make it, but making it meant getting the hell out of the worst part of the city. "Community" can have a broader meaning than neighborhood.

The case made here, in fact, is that geographical concentration only makes it easier to keep the blacks down. Politically, it simplifies exploitative gimmicks such as gerrymandering and contains black power well below the level at which it could get a share of the real action. Control of the ghetto is not nearly enough. Blacks have to get into the system at all levels, must be ready, now, to make alliances and arrangements with whites at all levels. Cutting the ghetto off politically would be the surest route to permanent colonial status.

In terms of economic power, the idea of keeping black money in the black community, not letting the honkies cart it out every night, makes good rhetoric. But the largest single need of would-be black entrepreneurs is capital, which, in the ghetto, is in short supply. What if the separatist premise were adopted by whites and they kept their capital close to home too?

The separatists divide on whether to let white industry come into the ghetto. Some are for it only if the proprietors will turn plants over to "the community." The question is all but academic. White industrialists are increasingly wary of the hostility they see in the ghetto and are seldom inclined to give their plants away. Modern factories, moreover, tend to sprawl because of automation and need more space, at lower land costs, than can be found in the innards of most cities; transporting materials in and products out is all but impossible on crowded ghetto streets. Even with government incentives, few economists see any prospect of reversing the trend that is taking industry—and jobs—to the suburbs.

Finally, if slum-ghetto residents decided to stay where they are and improve their neighborhoods, they would be engaging in a one-sided fight against history. Particularly in the older eastern cities, these neighborhoods became slums generations ago, before the blacks arrived in any substantial numbers. Through these generations, they have been the other side of the tracks, "red-lined" by mortgagers, insurers, and government agencies as undesirable areas and thus doomed to continuing cycles of decay. The relatively recent efforts to reverse the cycles have only proved how difficult the task is—so long as the slum-ghettos remain the only option open to their residents. No city has succeeded in improving slum-ghetto housing in any meaningful quantity at prices the residents could afford to pay. In part, the reasons have to do with the insufficiency of national programs directed to this purpose, but in larger part they reflect a historic stigma that can only be re-moved from these neighborhoods by major surgery.

If this sounds like white pessimism about black aspirations, consider the following account of a workshop on economics and black self-help, part of the 1968 black power conference in Philadelphia. It was written by Clarence Funnye, a black city-planner who is militant without being separatist, for the *Village Voice*.[3]

One delegate shouted that people didn't come hundreds of miles to hear jivetime clichés about ghetto gilding and economic development of ghettos while ghetto income continues down in both absolute and relative terms, blacks are locked into central cities while industries and jobs move out, and new in-dustrial development accelerates in all-white suburbs. A brother from Detroit angrily asked: "How in hell we're gonna talk about economic development when the bulk of black people are being separated by training or distance from jobs which have formed the base economy of black people? We going to just feed on each other?"

Alfred Rhodes shot back that those were "white men's fac-tories out there in the suburbs," and all hell broke loose. "What you mean white men's factories?" a brother from Chicago shouted. "When your government takes from tax money 40 billion bucks and gives it to some private airplane company to build some SST plane, baby that factory is yours no matter where he builds it—and you better start getting together and figure out some way to get out there and get some of that ac-tion."

The moderator called for order, but the assembly chorused "let's hear the brother," and the brother pressed on. "See how much land a factory takes up, how much vacant land is there in our communities? Man, just to build a totlot we have to tear down three houses and move 30 families. . . . Don't buy this—that just because you might want some clean air and green grass for your kids, that makes you some kind of imitation white man. Dig it, we ain't no more native to the ghetto than the white man is native to America. . . . All I say is we should check out the action wherever it is—we don't all have to be in the ghetto just to be brothers. Calling a prison a community don't make it so."

Who Speaks for Whom?

The appeal of separatism may be less hope in what it offers than despair of alternatives. If you were to stand outside of another's door, seeking admittance, and got only a hard stare of rejection with no move to turn the lock, if you returned time and again and met the same rebuff, sooner or later you would either kick the door in or go home, not to return until invited. Thus is it with blacks and racial integration.

Harold Fleming, president of the Potomac Institute, a Washington organization specializing in race relations, describes himself as an integrationist in the sense of one who works "for a truly open society in the hope that it will result in a living pattern and in mutual appreciation not bounded by race."[4] But what has given integration a bad name, Fleming has written,

> is not the hoped-for reality as just defined, but what has been done or not done in the name of an empty promise. To permit a trickle of accomplished Negroes to pass one by one through the screen of discrimination into honorary whitehood is not integration—and it is understandably resented. To deny desperately needed and wanted resources to existing ghettos on grounds that they will perpetuate segregation—this is not integration. To admit Negroes to situations in which they have no voice, in which total control rests in white hands—this is not integration. Since most of what is called integration consists of these three varieties, it is not surprising that many blacks have rejected it.

What is surprising, in fact, is how many blacks have not. To hear the militant separatists tell it, they have become the only legitimate spokesmen for the ghetto. Indeed, if rated by column inches in the white press, it would seem sometimes as if they were the only spokesmen. They are the ideologues, bright and articulate; they make good copy. Next to them, less-militant blacks look old and tired.

But there is evidence that their constituency, while growing, is not nearly so large as claimed. Measurements of black attitudes have become a periodic staple of the news media and have been supplemented by similar studies undertaken by university researchers. Notable examples have been three *Newsweek* surveys, the most recent one published in the summer of 1969; a CBS poll, telecast in the fall of 1968; a two-year study of Watts by a UCLA research team; and the University of Michigan survey for the Civil Disorders Commission, released in 1968 as a supplement to the commission's report. A careful comparative reading shows great diversity and flux in black opinion, but a consistent strain of allegiance to the goal of entry into the mainstream of American society. Most blacks, the surveys say again and again, want in rather than out.

The Michigan survey was the most extensive and, in many respects, the most interesting in its conclusions. The black respondents were asked a series of ten questions relating to separatism versus integration, and the number favoring the separatist position ranged from 5 to 18 per cent. Three questions related to the use of violence as a tactic, and only 6 to 15 per cent approved.

But the survey went on to portray the mood of the urban black as both complex and changing. "The most apparent fact," the Michigan report said, is that the mood is not yet revolutionary. "The great majority do not propose to withdraw from America; they want equal status in it. They do not talk of tearing down the economic and political institutions of the nation; they seek to share equally in the benefits. The majority—but in this no longer the *great* majority—are not despondent and without hope for the future." Of the respondents, a third disagree that there has been genuine progress. This third—representing more than a million Negroes in the fifteen cities surveyed, by a projection of the sample—"believe discrimination in employment and housing are major facts of life for Negroes today, facts of life that are not getting much better." Within this third is a smaller group, "small but not trivial in numbers," who feel violence to be necessary if change is to be achieved. The violent minority, says the report, "have the sympathy and perhaps to some extent the support of the larger minority discussed above. The most important fact about those inclined toward violence is that they are not an isolated band of deviants condemned by almost all other Negroes, but are linked to a much larger group by a common definition of the problems that beset the Negro in America."

The radical, separatist movement, moreover, may have strength beyond its numbers. "To deviate from a very widely held norm probably requires more conviction than to hold to it," the report notes. Also, the concentration of blacks in the cities provides the separatist spokesmen with "easy access to just the audience they wish to reach." There is evidence outside of the survey to indicate that they are making effective use of this access. Whether the militant voices speak for a black majority or not, as sociologist Nathan Glazer has pointed out, in the current debate "the moderate forces are silenced. . . . Whatever the size of the radical element, it has undoubtedly seized the political initiative."

The Michigan survey makes clear that the young, in particular, are listening. The percentage of teenage Negroes who believe in a separate black nation (11 per cent) is more than double the percentage of the elder generation. Nearly a third are ready to use violence to gain Negro rights. The degree to which this portends a long-term trend toward radicalism, the report points out, depends on the degree to which the teenagers retain their radical viewpoint as they grow older. The survey, which found a similar tendency toward violence in the young whites, suggests that it may be explainable "in terms of a conception of teenage masculine daring that has little to do with race." It may also mean the rise of a truly revolutionary generation; the report acknowledges that the survey offers no way to tell.

If Stokely Carmichael and H. Rap Brown are listened to, the report notes, it is because of "their emphasis on the serious difficulties Negroes face and [their] vociferous attribution of these difficulties to white America." The survey also presents evidence of a widespread response to that part of black power that encourages black pride. While 80 per cent of the black respondents disagreed that all ghetto stores should be Negro-owned, 94 per cent said that there should be more Negro businesses, and 70 per cent, that they should be favored by Negro customers. Ninety-six per cent said that "Negroes should take more pride in Negro history." And 42 per cent said that "Negro school children should study an African language"—striking support for a proposition that "a few years ago was scarcely discussed by most Negroes and still seems exotic and impractical to most white ears."

The assertion of black identity, the report says, is something quite different from separatism and well within the tradition of American pluralism: "It involves a commitment to the development of Negro identity as a valid basis for cultural life within a larger interracial and if possible integrated society." But the report tempers this enormously hopeful prospect with a warning: "Such a movement from race to ethnicity may help Negroes in a number of ways, but it does not promise quick relief to problems of perceived discrimination and unfair treatment."

The UCLA research team similarly found Watts residents to be "looking for tangible evidence that the nation has not lost its sense of commitment. . . . They are pondering the various solutions being debated within their own ranks. Their direction will be affected markedly by the economic, political, and social climate. If, for example, they discern a regressive climate that stresses increased police power as the answer . . . then the program of the extreme militants will of necessity find favor."[5] That program is revolution.

The message of the surveys, then, is not that the nation can relax, that the "good Negroes" are in charge. It is that the nation still has some time in which to keep its promise. Just now, it is not possible to say how much time. The surveys indicate that most blacks are still believers, but their faith won't keep forever. The young blacks—in the streets and in the colleges—show progressively less belief in the system and more in their own rhetoric.

There are, at this moment, ghetto leaders spreading the word to keep it cool. They are saying that there's no sense burning the community down when we're trying to build it up; that the people hurt by riots have been black people; that it's not time yet for revolution. They said the same thing in summer of 1968, with some effect.

But they will be listened to only so long as they produce. And to produce, they need more resources than the larger society, the white society, has been willing to provide. Whites who hold back are weakening these leaders' hands and hastening revolution. Whites who turn blacks away kill hope and help the cause of separatism.

In the deceptive quiet of early August, 1968, on a CBS-TV program called "Of Black America," James Turner, a young black instructor in political sociology at Northwestern University, lectures a study group. His subject is Denmark Vesey, who led an abortive slave insurrection in Charleston, West Virginia, just after the American Revolution. Denmark Vesey, Turner says, "walks the streets of the black community today. He is in the minds and the bosoms of young black men, who strive now with pride and dignity in the black community, who say that they will . . . struggle to transform their blight into a community. They will do it, or die trying."

Turner's image is replaced on the screen by that of Calvin Lockridge, also black, addressing what is described as a "training session." Lockridge is saying, "All revolutions are led by a hard core dissident group. And I think this is where we have to start. . . . And when we move, we'll move the masses of people around an issue. . . . There's a revolution going on. And anyone who doesn't join in, who is in the way . . . you have to treat him like a traitor or a spy. That means you kill him." There is no disagreement registered on the attractive, intelligent, black faces around the room.

Then the program's moderator—his name is George Foster and he, too, is black—comes in with the wrap-up: "Neither James Turner nor Calvin Lockridge would win any elections today. So far they represent only a minority of a minority. Yet their potential constituency can be found on any sidewalk in any slum . . . The question posed by increasing black activism is: Will white America respond before the few become the many?"

And the screen goes dim without an answer.

5

White
Power

While the nation's attention has been held by the ghetto disorders, another type of riot has been going on: in Milwaukee, in Brooklyn, in Cicero, Illinois, in Folcroft, Pennsylvania, and in the Kensington section of Philadelphia. These riots have been smaller in scale but no less intense: Violence continued for five days and nights in Kensington before police could bring it under control.

These rioters are white. In some instances, violence has followed a black family's attempt to move into a white neighborhood; in others, it has been a direct response to Negro demonstrations. After the Kensington riot, sociologist Murray Friedman, of nearby La Salle College, sought to identify its causes.[1] These are some of his findings:

Kensington is a community of 187,000 people, most of them Roman Catholic, about a third of first-, second-, or third-generation ethnic stock. It is an aging section of factories interspersed with small red-brick houses. Many are well-kept; others are run-down, as are most neighborhood facilities: Kensington gets nowhere near its share of Philadelphia's capital budget. Most Kensingtonians are unskilled or semi-skilled workers. Their median income is $300-to-$1,600 below that of the city as a whole.

Kensington, in other words, has much in common with the black North Philadelphia ghetto just to the east. But it looks at the ghetto with apprehension and resentment rather than fellow-feeling. The ghetto is slowly expanding into Kensington, and it was at one beachhead of this "invasion" that the rioting began.

Friedman observed that

Kensingtonians are beset by economic problems and status anxieties. The process of upward movement has been slow and hard fought. Frequently, the gains made are endangered by the possibility of loss of jobs, slow-down in the economy, or are drained off by inflation. One senses a feeling of displacement among the people living here, an ebbing of the jobs and pleasures that once characterized working-class life.

Friedman points out that "these anxieties are increased as they watch—in their opinion—the lawlessness of Negro violence in Watts and Detroit being rewarded by special federal and city efforts to aid the Negro." They read daily of private and public assistance "pouring into seemingly-favored Negro areas of the city." Emerging from a meeting, board members of a Lutheran settlement house in Kensington found the air had been let out of their car tires. One girl, caught running from the scene, was asked why she had done it; the girl replied, "I know what you were doing in there. You were planning to build a community center for the niggers."

Through black consciousness and black power, the Negro is trying to gain identity, but "the white Kensingtonian seeks to *maintain* his identity by keeping the Negro, a group just below him on the social scale, from overtaking him." Yet blacks and white Kensingtonians have one important characteristic in common: "Beyond their aggressive and seemingly self-confident behavior is an underlying feeling of powerlessness," Friedman says. "Here are people with severe problems they are unable to deal with, that the community is overlooking, and who find it difficult to take their place in an increasingly middle-class American society." The depression welded the two groups together with others to bring social reform. Now racial tensions have split them wide apart. They seem, in fact, on a collision course.

The white working class doesn't like what it sees happening in America—on the city streets, in the churches, on the college campuses, in the halls of government. In particular it doesn't like the way blacks are pushing up and in. Its resentments— and its resistance—have been building, unnoticed, for years, though they became especially strong during the period of the Great Society. Psychiatrist and author Robert Coles conducted a series of interviews among the white working class of Boston and, in the transitional year 1966, summarized what he was told: "What the Negro calls the civil rights movement in the north," said his respondents,

> is in fact an attempt to crowd out others, from schools, jobs, and opportunities of one sort or another; no one is entitled to anything "special," not when others have to sit by and get little or nothing; somehow the Negro is rather devious and clever, as well as half-witted and immoral, because he has managed to exact both sympathy and consistent help from people—the well born, the well educated—who have ignored the misery of other people for decades.[2]

These sentiments were expressed to Coles in blunt and angry language:

> The suburban housewives and the Ivy League students, they've gone poor-crazy, but only for the colored poor. . . . If the Negroes pull a switchblade on you and rob and steal you to the poorhouse, that means they've been persecuted, and we have to overlook everything they do and treat them as if they were God's gift to America.

And again:

> I just can't take what some of our priests are saying these days. They're talking as if we did something wrong for being white. . . . Everybody can't live with you, can they? Everybody likes his own. But now even the school people tell us we have to have our kids with this kind and that kind of person, or else they will be hurt, or something. . . . Who has to live with all this

and pay for it in taxes and everything? Whose kids are pushed around? And who gets called "prejudiced" and all the other sneery words? I've had enough of it.

Paul Cowan, following the Wallace campaign in mid-1968 for the *Village Voice*, heard much the same.[3] A machinist in Marlboro, Massachusetts:

I'm just a common man—I'm not smart enough to run this country—but I know there has to be an end to this looting and burning and rioting. Don't you think so? Do you think a man has a right to destroy the country when he isn't given something he hasn't earned in the first place? Do you think the government has the right to tax away my money and give it to somebody who doesn't want to work? And what about those students who have a chance for a good education and ignore their studies to make trouble?

And the wife of a chain-store floor manager:

You know, this whole country has gone berserk. The people I know are more frightened than they ever have been. And none of the politicians talk to them, none of them seem to know what to say anymore.

There is a great deal to be frightened about. The assassinations of John and Robert Kennedy, of Martin Luther King and Malcolm X have shaken the national mind to a degree only now becoming evident. Anyone living in a city struck by civil disorder, which means almost any major city, remembers the impact: fright approaching panic, distress, and depression are felt miles from the scene of violence. The cities, and their suburbs, come unhinged. Campus disruptions in both colleges and high schools, clashes between white youths and civil authorities are becoming increasingly violent. The rhetoric of protest is becoming more threatening. And the FBI index of reported crimes has risen very nearly 100 per cent in the 1960's, far beyond the capacity of the criminal-justice system to cope with.

In all this, there is nothing more fearful than the reaction to fear. Guns are everywhere: By the most conservative estimate of the Washington, D.C., police, there are 75,000 in the hands of the city's civilian population. Right-wing organizations—vigilantes, militiamen of resistance—are growing in number, becoming as outspoken in their militancy as the most radical blacks. Civil servants, in defense of their jobs and out of anger at the aggressiveness of their minority-group clients, are increasingly prone to strike—and each interruption of essential city services adds to the atmosphere of helplessness, of strife, of the world somehow falling apart.

Some of the white militants are in uniform. The police often share the ethnic and class roots of the working class and, thus, their fears and aversions. The police sometimes express these attitudes by meting out instant punishment to those they see as society's enemies—and there are now fewer voices in society insisting upon due process and restraint. The police are organizing too—in right-wing fraternal groups as well as in unions. The AFL-CIO has given its conditional blessing to formation of a police union on a national scale. Where already organized, the police have shown a willingness to use their power—the power to leave a frightened citizenry defenseless—to block such measures as external police review boards and community-relations programs.

George Wallace spoke directly to the frightened Americans, sought to play upon their fears. Some took comfort in his relative lack of success in the presidential vote, but the major reason may have been that his issues were co-opted. Richard Nixon spoke to these same people, called them the forgotten Americans, talked of law and order, counselled capitalism for the blacks and then largely ignored them. He was successful, but building an electoral majority and unifying a nation are two quite different tasks. The way he accomplished the first may make the second that much more difficult.

The Sins of the Liberals

One thing Mr. Nixon's majority cannot claim to be any longer is forgotten. Those demographer Richard Scammon described as "the unpoor, the unblack, and the unyoung" have not only elected a sympathetic President, they have also become the object of increasing, almost cultist concern on the part of academics, columnists, and other social commentators. Expressions of this concern usually are accompanied by castigation of the liberals for forgetting these people in the first place.

The argument goes like this: The white American of modest means has ample reason for dissatisfaction, even alienation. Taxes and prices have, for the past few years, risen faster than his income. He works hard at a job that may be boring, machinelike, yet still has trouble making ends meet. If he owns a home, the tax bite is especially severe: property taxes pay an inordinate share of the cost of local services. He doesn't feel he is getting much in return. The quality of these services has declined as budgets have risen; the streets aren't as well kept as they used to be, the schools not as good, the police not around when you need them, the garbageman only comes once a week. Government is getting larger and more remote. It may be doing a lot for somebody else—he has a hunch that a large chunk of his tax money is going for welfare —but it isn't doing much for him.

He worries about the general decline in authority and in morals. People, and especially kids, get away with too much. The kids have no respect for their teachers, the police, their parents. He reads about sex and drugs and fears his children may be trying both. They don't have much interest in the church, and small wonder. The church is changing—like everything else.

He feels himself, and is, on the front-line of integration and racial change. If the company begins favoring blacks, it may be his job (or the one he hoped his son or nephew would get) that they take. If the blacks begin moving out of the ghetto, it will be into his neighborhood, not the high-priced parts of the city or suburbs. He knows that the result will be to drive him out and values down, and the equity in his house may be his only savings. If the schools start busing, it will be his children who will be affected and, unlike the well-to-do, he cannot afford to send them to private schools to escape.

The white liberals, the argument continues, have abandoned this man in their fascination with the blacks. They preach integration, but they are not the ones who will pay its price. They preach social change exclusively in terms of black needs, thus increasing his resistance and strengthening his belief that the blacks are the favorites of society. And when he does resist, they dismiss him as a bigot.

That is about as far as the argument goes. The formerly forgotten American has demonstrated that he has the political and numerical strength to stop progress altogether; in some cities, he and his kind outnumber blacks three-to-one. If he cannot be somehow convinced or converted, at least his resistance must be lessened. The question becomes how to do this without, to turn the argument around, making poor blacks pay the price.

As a starting point, Nathan Perlmutter, of the American Jewish Committee, has suggested that liberals stop calling this man a racist.[4] "It would seem obvious enough that when arguing with a group whose conversion is imperative to the realization of our viewpoint, we do not name-call them," Perlmutter has written. "After all, bad-mouth a group as being a bunch of bigots, and do we really expect them to smile ruefully and allow as they hadn't quite seen themselves that way before, and from here on in, 'We'll do it your way'?"

Perlmutter's particular target is the "white racism" charge of the Civil Disorders Commission, and he quotes the black activist-intellectual Bayard Rustin as saying the charge "helped no one." But Rustin said a good deal more. In a pamphlet on the commission report, which was published by the American Jewish Committee itself, Rustin wrote:

> That report didn't say that Americans are racist. What the report was really saying was that the *institutions* of America brutalize not only the Negro but also whites who are not racists,

and who in many communities have to use racist institutions. When it's put on that basis, we know that the fundamental problem is not sitting around examining our innards, but getting out and fighting for institutional change.

Rustin is, of course, correct. The commission was talking about institutional racism rather than feelings that lurk deep in the minds and hearts of men. "White society is deeply implicated in the ghetto," said its report. "White institutions created it, white institutions maintain it, and white society condones it."

The difference between individual and institutional racism is explained by example in the Carmichael-Hamilton treatise on black power. When terrorists bomb a black church and kill five children, that is individual racism and is deplored. "But when in that same city—Birmingham, Alabama—five hundred black babies died each year because of the lack of proper food, shelter, and medical facilities . . . that is a function of institutional racism." When whites burn down a house bought by a Negro family, that is individual racism. "But it is institutional racism that keeps black people locked in dilapidated slum tenements, subject to the daily prey of exploitative slumlords, merchants, loan sharks, and discriminatory real estate agents." It is part of the system.

Without an understanding of this fact, the system will not be changed. Perlmutter complains that, "When the [Civil Disorders] Commission issued its finding that white racism was responsible for the past several summers of riots, liberals reacted to it with an enthusiasm that contrasted sharply with the cynicism with which they awaited it." But the commission's task was to identify the causes of civil disorders. To do so without reference to the way the system works against minorities (as some did fear the generally conservative commission might do) would have made its report incomplete, inaccurate, and even dishonest. To suggest now that racism be dropped from discussion of urban problems, so as not to offend the sensibilities of the resistant whites, is to render the discussion unreal. The blacks are listening too and they will notice the omission.

A more helpful suggestion is that the *emphasis* of the discussion be switched from race to problems shared by both blacks and whites. Murray Friedman put the point this way:

> One of the serious mistakes made by many liberals and persons of good will generally has been the effort to come to low-income white ethnic groups with a straight-out civil rights message on race relations, trying to convince these people that they should have more benevolent attitudes toward Negroes. That strategy has not worked.
>
> One of the really useful strategies one might consider instead is an approach to the basic problems of the area: problems of poor housing, inadequate mental health and recreational facilities, etc. Emphasis is needed on problems of deep concern to ethnic Americans, rather than on attempts to exhort and remold them into more pious positions and attitudes toward black people.

Friedman overstates somewhat: There is a difference between preaching benevolence and piety and asking one man to get off another's back. But there is much to recommend his strategy. Both blacks and whites are disadvantaged by economic injustice in our society, by the remoteness and inefficiencies of government, by revenue disparities that keep the cities poor, by environmental ills such as air and water pollution, haphazard development, inadequate transportation. These shared problems, as will be seen, may be the means of restoring a measure of peace between the striving blacks and resistant whites, perhaps one day once again bringing them together for common protest, common action. But first a single caveat must be inserted. Blacks and whites are not affected equally by urban problems. There is a large and continuing disparity in the degree to which blacks and whites are disadvantaged and the gap remains, to the blacks, the most galling fact of urban life.

Separateness and Unequality

Those who argue for keeping race in the background usually end up minimizing this disparity. Witness Perlmutter: "Schools of higher learning from the University of the City of New York to the Ivy League regularly release figures on the increasing percentages of black students who have been enrolled. Black Peter's long overdue educational favors are not unnoticed by white, untutored, and resentful Paul." Yet the Negro enrollments of public universities, by a 1969 count,[6] show that there are ninety-eight Pauls to every two black Peters. The conclusion is inescapable that race is a factor in the discrepancy. If race were to drop out of the discussion, the resistant whites would never know this fact; they would thus consider the redress of this particular injustice a "favor," as Perlmutter calls it, and could hardly be expected to understand or assent to efforts at increasing black enrollment.

And more: "The career expectations of the white male earning between $7,000 and $10,000 a year have been fixed since he reached the age of 35, when his debts, his family's size, and the disparateness between his skills and his ambitions combined to shape his tomorrows in the worn mold of his yesterdays. But Urban Coalitions, liberal rhetoric, Great-Society press releases are heard as being preoccupied solely with the Negro's upward occupational mobility." The point here is that Perlmutter's worn-mold-of-yesterdays poetry is mischievous. The white male can reach the $7,000 income level without sophisticated skills, as Perlmutter suggests, and without finishing high school, according to 1967 Census Bureau figures. The black male, by these same figures, has to get through more than a year of college.

In reality, the white working-class American may be more forgetful than forgotten. What society has done to equalize income and opportunity, while insufficient, has been done mainly for his benefit. The reforms begun in the New Deal lifted him to middle-class status. The labor movement has been largely his movement. Federal housing subsidies and federal income-tax exemptions have helped him become a homeowner. If the schools in his city are segregated, *de facto* or otherwise, it is his schools that invariably will have the better facilities and teachers, the higher budgets.

The blacks are still in a catch-up period, and they have a long way to go. Black income is rising—but blacks still only earn two-thirds of the average white family income and are three times as likely to be living in poverty. Black unemployment is declining—but remains nearly twice the white rate. Black jobs are at the low end of the scale of skills and rewards; there has been virtually no upward movement, in terms of occupational status, even in the enormously prosperous years 1966–68. The economic progress blacks have made, said the annual report of the President's Council of Economic Advisers in January, 1969, has been largely the result of this general prosperity—and could quickly and easily be wiped away by a general slowdown.

It would be unjust and unacceptable for society to say to the blacks: Let's just forget a few hundred years of history and start even. The blacks need and deserve not just opportunity but specific help in using opportunity. Nothing less will bring them close to equality; nothing less will end their alienation. Whatever strategies are devised to serve both black and white needs, and thus bring them together, there must be parallel compensatory strategies to remove the scars of past injustice.

It would make life and policy-making easier if this were not the case, if we could put race aside and just talk about nice, clean problems. But it is the case. However difficult, efforts must continue to make whites understand the disparity. They do not understand it now. The University of Michigan survey for the Civil Disorders Commission asked the white segment of its sample whether blacks with the same level of education were relatively better or worse off than they. An astounding 42 per cent said blacks were better off; 46 per cent said they were about the same; and only 5 per cent, that blacks were worse off. If nothing else, these figures indicate that it is no time to stop talking about conditions of life in the black slums and ghettos. Whether through honest ignorance or unwillingness to learn, whites simply do not know how bad it is. They will not act, or permit government to act, until they do.

Yet Perlmutter's point about the press releases and Friedman's about the liberal preachments are well taken. A lot depends on *how* the job of education, of advocacy, is done. The publicists of the Great Society, as we now realize and as noted in an earlier chapter, went about it in precisely the wrong way; they exaggerated both the size of urban programs and, at least by neglecting frequent mention of the fact that they would benefit whites as well as blacks, the concentration of the programs on minorities. Robert Kennedy seemed the only political figure of presidential size in recent years to be able to advocate help for the poor and minorities and still keep the allegiance of the working class. It may have been the fact that he was Irish and Catholic; it may have been that he gave off a sense of concern for all who felt left out of society. "I had the feeling that he really cared about people like us," a white television repairman in Framingham, Massachusetts, told Cowan of the *Village Voice*. The repairman switched to Wallace after Robert Kennedy's assassination.

The experiences of three mayors are instructive. Richard Daley of Chicago plays old-fashioned ethnic politics, giving out favors to whites and blacks alike (if not quite evenly) in return for allegiance to his powerful and monolithic machine. The new blacks, not part of the old machine, are rebuffed. Richard Daley honestly could not comprehend the Chicago civil disorders of 1968; his violent reaction, suggesting that adult looters be killed and young looters "maimed," was as much hurt and bewilderment as it was innate viciousness. One of these days Daley's Chicago may blow higher than a kite, and he still will not understand why.

John Lindsay of New York made clear his feeling for ghetto residents' problems in his famous street walks and a hundred other ways. New York stayed relatively cool through four summers, which will remain, whatever happens from now on, a major achievement. But John Lindsay neglected his other ethnic fences, gave the impression that he cared primarily for the minority poor. John Lindsay's priorities were in order, but the image he gave these priorities may have cost him his political future.

Kevin White of Boston, an acknowledged novice at city government when he took office, had an initial instinct that served him well. From the beginning, he was careful to apportion his attention to both black and white ethnic neighborhoods. He could be found walking the streets of the Roxbury ghetto, but he also was seen playing basketball with Italian kids in a North End schoolyard. When White instituted a network of "little city halls" to bring government closer to the neighborhoods, he was meticulously even-handed in where he put them.

Kevin White's Boston may blow too: Given the present level of urban resources, none of these three mayors can do enough for either whites or blacks. But Boston seems to be a less dangerously divided city than when he took office. The lessons for urban political leaders are (1) be, and seem, responsive to the neighborhoods, white and black; (2) don't talk about the needs of either without talking about the needs of both; and (3) if the blacks require, for a time at least, a higher priority, don't issue press releases about it. The same advice might be offered, in slightly different form, to presidents.

Beyond style, there remains the substance of Friedman's proposed strategy: to find problems that blacks and whites share and, perhaps one day, can unite to solve. Some can be small and simple things that make a large difference in daily life: refuse collection, street repair, good bus service. Other, larger matters of national programs and policies are dealt with in the remaining portion of this book. Most will require a willingness to assign a far larger share of national resources to the solution of urban problems. As long as the pie is of inadequate size, competition for slices will be fractious and bitter. Blacks and whites in the cities will not soon come together in frustration. They might in the hope of accomplishment, a hope that our present national priorities render remote.

The new militancy among working-class whites could, in the end, help bring about the redirection of priorities. To date, their role has been mainly negative and defensive, directed against the black enemy and his incursions. The second- and third-generation hyphenated Americans have not tended to turn government to solve their problems. But Monroe W. Karmin of the *Wall Street Journal* reported, in the spring of 1969, that the white ethnic organizations were regrouping to go after their share of what government was giving out. Their younger members, as one Polish elder told him, "are more interested in Pittsburgh than Warsaw." The motivation may still have to do with race, but the significance is that they are acting as aroused, aggrieved citizens rather than vigilantes. In Boston, similarly, the program of little city halls has helped stimulate awareness in some white ethnic neighborhoods that they have problems government can do something about, if enough pressure is put on.

This pressure, added to that of the blacks and raised to national scale, could turn the nation around. The blacks and working-class whites don't have to like each other. They do have to be willing to deal with each other, to make trade offs and, occasionally, common cause. That is the way a pluralistic society works and perhaps the only way a single society can be achieved. For the enemy of the black man in the cities is not the working-class white, nor vice versa. The enemy is the system that denies to both their share of society's rewards and promises and, in the process, pits them against each other. Together they can change the system.

6

The

Goal

America has lived its history in irony. No nation began its life with loftier statements of principle and purpose, or renewed its commitment to them with more oratorical regularity. All men, created equal, would live in a nation that was one and indivisible, exercising their inalienable right to life, liberty, and the pursuit of happiness. Government would secure and perfect these guaranteed blessings, promoting justice, tranquility, and the general welfare.

The irony has been in the exceptions. The "all men" deemed equal by the Declaration of Independence did not include the nearly one-sixth of the new nation's population that was in slavery. When the Constitution made its promises to "ourselves and our posterity" it referred specifically to the white proprietors of America. It took generations to bring an end to slavery, thus giving blacks the right to their lives. They are still seeking liberty, and have made their largest gains in civil rights in the few short years since World War II. The suggestion that the pursuit of happiness implies certain social rights—free access to jobs and housing, for example—is recent enough to remain, for many, a radical concept.

The poor have been similarly excluded from these guarantees. Promotion of the general welfare began on a large scale only during the Depression, nearly 150 years after the Constitution was adopted, when suddenly it seemed that almost everyone was poor. Until then, the operative principle had been survival of the fittest, with poverty regarded as the result of defects in character. It was left to a few reformers to point out the difficulty of pursuing happiness on an empty stomach. Even today, between 10 and 14.5 million Americans, by estimates of a 1968 citizens' commission, go to bed hungry in a nation rich beyond its founders' dreams.[1] There has been virtually no change in the percentage distribution of income since war completed, for most, the New Deal's program for recovery.

What must be understood if America is to find its way out of its current domestic crisis is that these exclusions have been more than mere failings of the democratic system. It is not as if the nation had fully adopted the goals stated by its founders, but somehow fallen short of meeting them in the press of day-to-day affairs. These goals were modified and abrogated by general consent, as if by tacit amendment passed by a huge and silent constitutional convention. The poor and the blacks have been set apart from the rewards of American democracy by ignorance of, and indifference to, the full extent of their exclusion, but they have also been set apart by cold and calculating intention.

The remedies to poverty, for example, "are fairly well known," political scientist Harry C. Bredemeier has written.[2] "They are not effectively applied because poverty remains, on net balance, profitable to those not in it." The rewards of poverty to the nonpoor include a low-paid labor force to do the difficult and dirty work of society. The costs of poverty to the nonpoor, says Bredemeier, "are neither very great nor sharply perceived."

In 1964, Adam Walinsky, a top aide to Robert Kennedy, wrote in an article called "Keeping the Poor in Their Place: Notes on the Importance of Being One-Up":

> In present-day America, the middle-class is defined largely by the fact that the poor exist. Doctors are middle-class, but so are bookkeepers; factory workers vacation with lawyers, drive

bigger cars than teachers, live next door to store-owners, and send their children to school with the children of bank tellers. In a middle-class so diffuse, with almost no characteristic common to all, middle-class income, education, and housing are what the poor do not have. If the present poor should become middle-class, no meaning would remain to that phrase. . . . The middle-class knows that the economists are right when they say that poverty can be eliminated if we only will it; they simply do not will it.[3]

Walinsky may be a bit hard on the middle class, millions of whom are sympathetic to the poor in the abstract. The problem is, in large part, that they seldom see the poor in the particular. The most precise analysis of this phenomenon remains Michael Harrington's *The Other America.*[4] The transformation of the American city into metropolis has meant that the poor are "increasingly isolated from contact with, or sight of, anybody else," Harrington said. "The failures, the unskilled, the disabled, the aged, and the minorities are right there, across the tracks, where they have always been. But hardly anyone else is."

Joseph Lyford, of the Center for the Study of Democratic Institutions, speaks of "our remarkable ability to endure other people's acute discomfort." Lyford does not mean that the average American will deny a starving man a crust of bread; rather, he means that our society endures poverty by keeping it out of sight and mind, whether consciously or through indifference. Poverty itself has been permitted to become an American institution in poignant and permanent contrast to the characteristic affluence of the American way of life.

Prejudice, as suggested earlier, has been likewise institutionalized. The process began with slavery, deemed necessary for the economic progress of America as a colony and then as a young nation. Later, racial segregation and discrimination became essential elements of the southern society and economy, almost as rigid, almost as destructive, almost as profitable as slavery. The rest of the nation looked the other way, except for the occasional expression of condescending disapproval. Then the blacks came North, and the white institutions stiffened. As potential competitors, blacks were kept out of business, out of unions, out of politics, and out of white neighborhoods—which meant out of white schools. Their exclusion was, and is, part of the system.

In his prophetic book *Crisis in Black and White,* Charles Silberman delivered a harsh but accurate assessment of the situation.[5] "The tragedy of race relations in the United States," wrote Silberman, "is that there is no American Dilemma. White Americans are not torn and tortured by the conflict between their devotion to the American creed and their actual behavior. They are upset by the current state of race relations, to be sure. But what troubles them is not that justice is being denied but that their peace is being shattered and their business interrupted."

Nation Divisible

Thus it is that when the Civil Disorders Commission proposes that America move against poverty and prejudice, when it calls upon the nation to "realize the promise of a single society—one nation, indivisible—which yet remains unfulfilled," it is not simply indulging in patriotic rhetoric. It is introducing a national goal that is both radical, in the context of American history, and controversial, in the context of current urban conflict.

There are both blacks and whites ready to contest it vigorously. The blacks are separatists to whom division of society is, if not an ultimate goal, the most effective current tactic. The dream of a single society, as they see it, is so unattainable as to be harmful to the cause of black progress. The rhetoric of the democratic process is a delusion. "The fourth of July is yours, not mine," said the Negro abolitionist Frederick Douglass to an Independence Day audience in 1852. "To drag a man into the grand illuminated temple of liberty, and call upon him to join you in joyous anthems, is inhuman mockery." Added Carmichael and Hamilton 115 years later, "We understand the rules of the game and we reject them."

On the white side are those who fear they would be obliged to give up something if the have-nots are to be raised to full participation in a single, unified society. In some cases, the loss might be money (if only through increased taxation); in others, political power; in still others, that most prized of American possessions, status. The blacks, as long as the myth of their inferiority can be preserved, give millions of marginal whites someone to look down upon—someone whose status is, by general (white) agreement, automatically low. "The tragedy of the American Negro," Nathan Glazer said in *Encounter*, "is that everything he touches or can touch becomes to some measure defiled with the notion that, as long as it is something *he* achieves in a white man's society, it is in some measure undignified."

Is creation of a single society worth the costs? The only way that question can be answered is by examining the alternatives, which the Civil Disorders Commission did in its report. Step by step, the commission projected the future consequences of three possible choices, one of which amounts to inaction.

The first choice the commission called "present policies." Following this path, the nation would continue to devote about the same percentage of the resources it now provides to programs that help the poor and the minorities in the cities; it would do nothing more than at present to lessen segregation. This choice, the commission suggested, would be the equivalent of inaction: "Federal programs have been so small that they fall short of effective enrichment [of the ghetto]," it said. "As for challenging concentration and segregation, a national commitment to this purpose has yet to develop."

If this were the nation's choice, the commission continued, "a rising proportion of Negroes in disadvantaged city areas might come to look upon the deprivation and segregation they suffer as proper justification or for violent protest for extending support to now isolated extremists who advocate civil disruption by guerrilla tactics." White retaliation could follow, starting a spiral that "could quite conceivably lead to a kind of urban apartheid with semimartial law in many major cities, enforced residence of Negroes in segregated areas, and a drastic reduction in personal freedom for all Americans, particularly Negroes." So much for present policies.

The second option, which the commission termed "enrichment," would entail increasing the extent of help given the ghettos and their residents but doing nothing to end segregation. The immediate effect of this choice could be to reduce tensions, although, as the commission warned, the announcement of new programs might raise more hopes than such programs could satisfy. But it was the long-term effect that concerned the commission: the creation of two separate societies, which could never be equal. The U.S. economy "and, particularly, the sources of employment" are white; continued economic separation, therefore, "could only relegate Negroes to permanently inferior incomes and economic status." In education, the commission accepted those research findings that "suggest that both racial and economic integration are essential to educational equality for Negroes." In housing, enrichment could improve the quality of shelter in the ghetto but "could not provide Negroes with the same freedom and range of choices as whites with equal incomes," choices that extend to city and suburbs alike.

Enrichment, the commission acknowledged, could reduce the prospect of civil disorders for as long as twenty years, depending on the scale of the new programs. But, it warned, "men are not necessarily placated even by great absolute progress. The controlling factor is relative progress—whether they still perceive a significant gap between themselves and others whom they regard as no more deserving." In twenty years, that gap might be much wider—and all but impossible to close.

With the third choice, "integration," enrichment of the ghetto would be only an interim step toward the final goal of "achieving freedom for every citizen to live and work according to his capacities and desires, not his color." This is the only choice the commission found acceptable if this nation is to ward off either greatly increased violence or permanent relegation of the American Negro to second-class status.

In calling its third choice "integration," the commission took pains to say the definition did not include forced movement of blacks out of the cities. Still, integration retains the ring of something that is done *to* somebody, whether that somebody is a black who might be resettled or a white child who is bused to a school across the city. A more apt term would be desegregation. What has to be done to unify the nation is to remove the barricades that presently cut it into racial and economic enclaves, barricades that have been created by poverty and prejudice.

A single society would be one in which all Americans were free to move where they pleased or stay where they were—and, if they were black and chose to stay in the city, to do so without paying the penalty of their neighborhood being the worst neighborhood in town. Enrichment means removal of the "color-tax" of bad housing, bad schools, and poverty, which society has imposed on the ghetto. Desegregation means freedom. Together they could be the basis for building "one nation, indivisible," the goal to which all of the nation's urban strategies must be consciously shaped.

Programs Versus Policy

All of this has more than philosophical significance. In the spring of 1969, in an address that was decidedly encouraging for its vision, presidential adviser Daniel Patrick Moynihan pointed out that while urban-related *programs* have proliferated, there exists no national urban *policy* in the sense that there is a foreign policy. Putting aside the question of whether that foreign policy is good or bad, it is at least explicit and is based on continuing analysis and public discussion of where America stands in the world, where it wants to go, and how it can get there. Long-range objectives and short-range actions and strategies are debated by the press and political candidates.

The same can hardly be said of the domestic side. Moynihan's address represented very nearly the first time anyone that close to the center of power had even attempted to suggest what a national urban policy might be. The Urban Affairs Council, which he heads in the Nixon Administration, is, similarly, the first creature of the executive branch to be given a mandate to talk urban in over-all policy terms. Until now, the federal response to urban problems has been spasmodic and fragmented. Program has been piled on program; each has had its own objectives, its own redundancies, its own constituents and enemies. There have been no coherent, comprehensive national urban goals, no policy framework within which to examine programs. Therefore, there has been no debate.

The most recent case in point was the 1968 presidential campaign. Beginning at the two major party conventions, urban problems were largely relegated first to platform subcommittees, then to expert "task forces," hardly surfacing in the public confrontations. The candidates searched for phrases and positions that would turn on one group without turning off others. They ended by focusing on specific programs and small ideas that, for one reason or another, touched a nerve, brought audience response. The large issues—the ones that were, in 1968, well on their way to tearing the nation apart—were for the most part dealt with in random generalities.

One pathetic example was the Job Corps program. In one of his few urban specifics, Richard Nixon said during the campaign that he thought the program a prime candidate for extinction, apparently on grounds of its cost (which he exaggerated). The Job Corps was a modest little effort at best, based on the premise that to prepare inner-city teenagers for useful futures, it was necessary not just to give them job training but also to give them other skills of urban living. This could best be done, the theory went, away from their own neighborhoods where there was already so much working against them.

To do so, of course, was more costly than simple job training, but also, according to OEO evaluations of the program, more productive. It meant, too, that Job Corps centers were in many cases located outside the big cities, near suburbs and small communities that often were less than delighted to have the trainees as neighbors. Presidential Counsel Arthur Burns may have had this in mind when, commenting on the Nixon Administration's subsequent cutback of these centers in favor of smaller ones in the cities, he criticized the removal of the trainees from their "natural environments." The cutback took the form of eliminating 59 of the 113 Job Corps centers, reducing the number of trainees from 35,000 to 24,000, and closing the gates to 3,000 recruits awaiting assignment.

The point is not so much the wisdom of this move—although it is hard to see how it will decrease tensions among inner-city teenagers—but how grandly free from strategic thought it seemed. Mr. Nixon did not emphasize, in the public phases of his campaign, the need for clearing out the present tangle of federal manpower policies, nor, for that matter, did his opponent. There was never any real debate over how best to cope with the problem of selective unemployment in the midst of prosperity; over what kind of strategy could give hope to the nearly one third of nonwhite youngsters in the cities who were out of jobs; over whether part of the strategy should involve taking them out of their decidedly unnatural environments. Mr. Nixon simply reached into this can of worms, plucked out the Job Corps, and promised to squash it. With the exception of a few late speeches by Hubert Humphrey— too late and too carefully hedged—that was about the level of urban discussion in the 1968 campaign.

It was about the level that foreign policy discussion reached in the 1930's, before World War II made both isolationism and pacifism unfeasible. Much of the nation, in those years, was able to ignore the increasingly clear threats posed by the totalitarian nations of Europe and Asia, just as most of the nation is now able to ignore the threats at home. One can only hope that the ending of internal isolationism will not require a domestic Pearl Harbor.

The scale of the discussion must be raised beyond specific crises, beyond specific programmatic responses, to the level of national policy. At that level, the matter of goals, of objectives, becomes crucial. As a beginning, the nation must decide—truly decide—whether it wants to be one society or stay as two, because that decision affects nearly every aspect of national urban policy, nearly every potential strategy. Without this decision, there is little hope of replacing the present scattering of programs with a coherent policy; indeed, the unwillingness to face this decision may be one reason for the policy vacuum.

It would be quite possible, even easy, to choose the two-society alternative and ratify our present *ad hoc* apartness. On the one hand, we would need to adopt a set of urban pacification programs to reduce the current level of tensions. This is essentially the Civil Disorders Commission's enrichment choice. Many of our present programs would be well suited to the pacification effort, requiring only additional funding. Our housing and community-development programs, in fact, are already oriented toward improvement *within* the ghettos. So is the community-action program of the War on Poverty, by and large. We might need some additional legislation along the lines of the widely discussed community self-determination bill introduced in the Ninetieth Congress, which, in essence, would have given the ghetto a corporate structure to undertake profit-making enterprises and the delivery of social services with direct federal help. But most of the necessary pacification measures are, in one form or another, already on the books. Most were enacted with precisely this purpose in mind.

On the other hand, to make the two-societies choice stick, we would also need urban containment programs. At first this requirement might seem to present constitutional difficulties, but they are more theoretical than real. We always have the option of amending the Constitution, although it isn't really necessary to go to all that trouble: We can achieve, have achieved, a high degree of containment just by keeping hands off. The real estate interests and housing industry, without too much direct government help, have efficiently demarked the two societies' boundaries. We could even keep the federal fair-housing law on the books, just so appropriations for enforcement stay at their present level. Similarly, the South has, over the past eleven yerrs, shown us how to forestall a mixture of the two societies in the schools. In the North, that problem is taken care of automatically so long as residential boundaries are maintained.

Further, we could take positive steps to see that opposition to containment remains ineffective. The separatists already are well on their way to political control in the black community, despite their limited numbers, and it would not take too much additional help from the white society to strengthen their hold. Many whites already seem willing, even anxious to prove their relevance by dealing only with the most militant separatist leaders. Again, the community self-determination bill, if it could be revived, offers an ingenious device for delivering federal funds into the hands of a few such leaders without the confusion of elections, thus assuring the permanence of their reign. Mr. Nixon has spoken out strongly for black self-help and self-determination; he has shown considerable caution about actions that would cause the two societies to merge.

What is written above is not parody: The two societies choice really would be that easy. We really are that far along, without ever having made the choice explicit. Perhaps it might be more accurate to say that we are moving toward the point of making our refusal to choose explicit. White resistance to integration, black rejection of it, the rise of radicalism of the left and right, the disdain for liberalism—all are being expressed (sometimes shouted) more openly, challenged less effectively.

From the viewpoint both of black progress and of the nation's future stability the case for a single society has already been made. As stated in the Civil Disorders Commission report: Separate can never be equal; choicelessness is as damaging as powerlessness; most blacks want in, not out, of the system; pacification programs can ease deprivation but would, over time, widen the gap between black and white progress; life in a house divided is neither pleasant nor safe. But to these arguments a further point should be added: The more explicit our decision to remain divided, the more democracy will be in danger from without and within. The day a majority publicly asserts to this decision, something essential in this country will have died: America will no longer be able to make its claims on the hopes of men for freedom. And on that day, America will become, explicitly, both an enemy and a threat to the surging, growing Third World of nonwhite nations.

Premises and Policy

The goal of a single society will not be so easy to achieve. It will require changes in priorities, programs, and institutions as well as in attitudes. The barriers to oneness are highest in the cities, where they are buttressed by the structural and financial inability of local government to respond to citizens on either side, where competing groups live in close proximity and feelings are rubbed raw by the abrasiveness of the environment. But the changes must go beyond the cities to the national government and beyond present crises to the accommodation of future growth.

A national urban policy based on this goal must, first of all, deal with both the aggressiveness of black pride and the militancy of white power. The most immediate priority is to relieve the deadliness of the slum-ghetto environment and ease the explosive disparity between the black and white experience of the city. This must be accomplished, moreover, in a way that builds self-regard and self-reliance: To the greatest possible extent, the residents of the slums and ghettos must draw the specifications and carry out the work.

The same incentives should be offered the white neighborhoods of the city to meet the needs that they identify. The slums and ghettos have gotten organized to press their demands; the white neighborhoods should be encouraged to do so too. Local government, while setting budgetary priorities according to the depth of needs, should be evenhanded in its willingness to listen and respond. Whatever degree of decentralization this requires of city hall should apply citywide. No program should be installed to serve a single group or neighborhood, even though the uses of programs may vary, should vary, with the neighborhoods' differing degrees of need.

To be responsive, local governments will need more money. Eventually it must come down from the federal government—given the present tax system, that is where the public money gathers—but it should come down with fewer and larger strings. The cities should have maximum feasible flexibility in use of the money within a framework of over-all national purposes. The federal government should identify those problems that are national, such as poverty, and pay the bill for them. It should encourage, through the large strings on its money, the reorganization of lower levels of government so that for each scale of problem there is a matching level of response.

Nationally, the goal of a single society requires a policy of building choice. Programs to help the disadvantaged catch up —in jobs, income, housing, education, health—should be color-blind and focused on the individual. To the greatest extent possible, the individual should carry whatever subsidies he requires with him wherever he goes, so that his very presence does not constitute a burden on the local community. The federal government, with and through the states, must take a positive hand in the direction of future growth, in the deployment of land and population. The objective should be to induce and encourage patterns of urban development that end the waste of random growth, so that class or color no longer preordain where Americans shall live.

These are the premises for a national urban policy. Some specifics of such a policy are suggested in the following chapters.

7

Starting

Points

James W. Rouse is a Baltimore mortgage banker and developer who is building the new community of Columbia, Maryland, halfway between his home city and Washington. Rouse said once that the planning of Columbia was based on a simple question: What kind of community would encourage a child living in it to attain maximum growth as a human being? Rouse saw to it that every step of the process of Columbia's planning and development was tested against this question. A similar question can help put the task of urban development in human perspective: What would the child born today in a Harlem hospital need to grow into a fully functioning member of society?

He would need, as a beginning, the presence of a mother and father, something of a luxury at present to many Harlem children. The father would need a steady job that pays a living wage and assurance, if he should become ill or disabled, that the family will continue to have a decent income without loss of dignity.

The child would need health care, especially in the early months when his chances of survival are half those of white children in the city. When he grows old enough to play outside, he should have a park or playground somewhere nearby; it should be safe for him to play on the sidewalks, too, without the threat of contaminating contact with crime or degeneracy.

He should feel protected, not threatened, by the sight of a policeman on the corner. He should feel welcome in his world, free to move about outside his neighborhood, later on, without rebuff.

If his parents have grown up in deprivation, he will need an education that begins early, one that encourages pride and achievement and aspiration. School should give him both a sense of his own heritage and the chance to encounter the full mixture of people and ideas that comprise the society of which he will be part. He should also have the chance to take his education as far as his interest and abilities carry him. And he should be assured that education, once gained, will not be wasted. The child would need, above all, confidence that he can make a future.

These needs are not extravagant. They are fulfilled, as a matter of course, for many children born into America. But they are denied to most children born into the Harlems of America and are achieved for other children, in other parts of the city, only at the price of their parents' continual struggle. Rouse described his goal for Columbia as a "nourishing environment." That is not the kind of environment the city presently offers.

The first objective of a national urban policy, then, is to meet these basic needs. To do so successfully enough to change the lives of the city's children requires that all of these needs be acted upon at once; the defeating problems faced by the Harlem child are inextricably related one to another. Yet it is necessary to begin somewhere, to cut into the web in which the cities' residents are caught. This chapter offers three proposed starting points.

1. *Improvement of the everyday environment.* The visible condition of impoverished or marginal neighborhoods is a constant reminder to the residents of where they stand in society. If one's dwelling is shabby or worse; if the streets go unswept and the garbage uncollected; if these rubbished streets are punctuated with abandoned shells of buildings and cars; if play spaces are scarce and unkempt, the environment

does more than assault the senses of sight and smell. It assaults the spirit, especially that portion of the spirit where self-regard is built.

The inclination is to curse the neighbors (which is a little like cursing oneself), or the garbagemen's union, or the mayor. Though it is less satisfying, in reality the curses should be directed at the system, the ways public monies are collected and distributed, the ways public programs are planned and run. It is the system that litters these streets and lets these buildings decay to the point of abandonment.

To begin with, the mayor does not have the money to do much about it. "The federal government stole the goose that lays the golden eggs when the Sixteenth Amendment authorizing a graduated income tax was passed," Senator Joseph Clark, a former mayor, said during the Ribicoff Committee hearings. "Corporate and individual income taxes seek out the main earning streams of the economy, wherever they happen to lead." At the beginning of the New Deal, local governments collected over half of all tax revenues. Now they collect less than 10 per cent.

Once the money gets to Washington, getting it back is not easy. In 1965, the Census Bureau conducted a special revenue survey of the nation's thirty-eight largest metropolitan areas. They amount to less than a seventh of the total number of metropolitan areas, but, among them, account for 40 per cent of the population—and two-thirds of federal income-tax revenues. Together, the local governmental agencies in the thirty-eight areas—cities, suburbs, counties, as well as school, fire, and other districts—raised roughly three out of every four dollars they spent. In direct aid, Washington supplied only 2.4 per cent of their total revenues.

"The great economic anachronism of our time," economist John Kenneth Galbraith has said, providing a motto for every big-city mayor, "is that economic growth gives the federal government the revenues while, along with population increase, it gives the states and especially the cities the problems. The one unit of government gets the money, the other gets the work." What Moynihan, in his urban policy speech, called "the basic equation of American political economy" is that every 1 per cent rise in the GNP increases the federal government's income by 1.5 per cent—and that of city governments by .5 to .75 per cent. And so the gap goes.

Every rise in the GNP also increases the cost of everything the city buys or does. The city is hit, like any household, by the impact of inflation. So are its employees, many of whom are now unionized and thus able to enforce their demands for cost-of-living raises by tying city services in knots. John Lindsay's defeat in the primary election may not have been the result alone of riots or racial tensions, but remembrance, as well, of the dark days that the sanitation workers struck and garbage rotted at the curb or of the other days when snowdrifts remained on the streets until they turned black because, the mayor charged, these same workers shunned overtime. The wage demands of public employees, moreover, have become competitive: The firemen want as much as the police, the sanitation workers as much as the firemen, and so on down the line, creating the city's own internal inflationary spiral.

The shortage, as Lindsay has pointed out, is felt not just in the capital budget, by which the city rebuilds itself, but in the operating budget, by which the city is run. It is a shortage of money to pay salaries, maintain buildings, sweep the streets, clear the snow. Newark, in late 1968, was not just out of money to build new libraries—it was out of money to keep the libraries it already had open. The Newark situation was saved not so much by additional public revenues as by an eleventh-hour contribution from private funds. Similarly, Philadelphia considered closing its schools early in 1969, although it had the buildings and the teachers. What it didn't have was money to pay for building maintenance and teachers' salaries.

The condition of some urban neighborhoods, then, reflects, not just the poverty of their residents but the poverty of the

city as well. There may be no more purely local function than
street sweeping, but the fact the streets go unswept reflects
a national revenue imbalance that requires a national remedy.

The federal remedies attempted so far have been limited to
individual grant-in-aid programs, most of which are larger in
concept than in results. Urban renewal was supposed to pay
for making old neighborhoods new; as has been seen, it
foundered on the failure of related programs to increase suffi-
ciently the supply of low-income housing. These programs are
now beginning to be enlarged. Urban renewal has been
streamlined, and the Model Cities program has been installed
to bring environmental improvement under an umbrella that
includes social and economic programs.

But it will take enormous amounts of time before anything
visible happens. The 3,700-plus days that it took, according
to the federal task force in Oakland, to process a typical urban-
renewal project amounts to *more than ten years*. The everyday
environment of a marginal neighborhood can decline a great
deal in ten years; its decline is accelerated once the neighborhood is designated an urban-renewal area. If anything, delays
between conceiving and executing physical improvement programs have increased recently because of rising demands for
citizen participation. In many cities, these programs are virtually stalemated by disputes over who should represent the
community and what role they should play.

More of the delays, however, result from the federal government's approach to apportioning funds. The city in search of
federal money has to follow a bewildering, and sometimes con-
tradictory, set of specifications and instructions for each
separate program. "I use 90 per cent of my time getting the
money and only 10 per cent spending it for the purpose intended," said a Boston renewal official recently. The mayor of
Oakland, at the Ribicoff hearings, called this "the application
game." Many cities, he said, hire full-time personnel to do
nothing but submit applications for any and every federal
program in sight. The applications that are successful wind
up determining a city's improvement plans.

When the money arrives, it usually is tightly wrapped in a maze of small strings, shalls and shall-nots wound around it by a vigilant Congress or a nervous federal bureaucracy. This has been especially constricting to federal programs for housing rehabilitation, which, at one time, were thought of as the most promising alternative to the federal bulldozer: Instead of being razed and replaced, blighted housing was to be repaired so that the neighborhood would not be dislocated or its residents removed. Thus far, this approach has had exceedingly limited success. In most cases, the cost of rehabilitation has been such that the residents, who must move while the work is done, cannot afford to return.

Planner Charles Abrams, one of the sages of the housing field, pins much of the rehabilitation problem squarely on local building codes and FHA regulations. He came to this viewpoint while doing a housing study for Philadelphia, where he found a large supply of single-family homes on the market at prices of $1,500 to $5,000.[1] When these homes were bought by the local housing authority and rehabilitated, the ultimate price, at cost, was $12,300. The reason, said Abrams, was contained "in some 26 pages of housing authority specifications. A good oil heater, for example, had to be replaced by a gas heater; all wallpaper had to be removed irrespective of its condition; unless walls were crack-free, new plastering was mandatory; dry walls were unacceptable," and so on. In short, Abrams said, "each house had to be gutted regardless of whether it was in satisfactory condition."

The impression should not be left that the condition of the poorer urban neighborhood remains stagnant while the mayors and the federal agencies play the application game. To the contrary, it steadily moves toward deterioration until, when it reaches a certain point, mortgages and insurance become hard to get, and, one by one, the landlords simply let building maintenance slide. The occasional exception makes improvements at the risk of having his already high taxes raised. Eventually he too is defeated by the cycle of decay.

In New York City, where every cycle seems to move at maximum speed, some current estimates place the rate of building abandonment at ten times the rate of new housing construction for low- and moderate-income families. (A few years ago, New York went so far as to try a receivership program under which it took over hazardous buildings, made repairs, and billed the owners. In only 11 of the first 120 cases did the owners take their buildings back.) Rutgers University economist George Sternlieb said during Senate committee hearings on the 1968 housing bill that he had found a similar slippage of housing in Chicago, Newark, and other older cities. He called it "a situation of dynamic disintegration."

A starting point toward reversal of this cycle would be to put federal money into the hands of the cities to maintain these neighborhoods in a livable condition. It would not be a dramatic program, nor a vast one, and the end result would be nothing a plaque could be affixed to. But it could build something more important than monuments, namely individual and community pride.

The money would be provided without small strings, but with a couple of big ones. The cities would not be able to use it for things they are already doing, but only to expand existing services or install new ones (verifiable by a simple post-audit). The residents of the neighborhoods involved would choose and plan the projects and, if unemployment exceeded a set percentage, have first chance at doing the work.

The projects would be small things that make a visible difference in the life and appearance of the neighborhood. The funds could be used for additional street maintenance or garbage collection, for new benches for the streets or parks, for playground equipment, for trash baskets, They could finance removal of abandoned buildings owned by the city and replacement of the buildings with vest-pocket parks or playgrounds. They could pay for the towing away of abandoned cars.

Most important—because one's dwelling place is the most

crucial element of the everyday environment—the money could go into modest rehabilitation projects designed not to bring housing to middle-class suburban standards, but simply to make it habitable. Such work would include repairs but not major alterations. The purchase of needed appliances, including air conditioners, would be permitted at the discretion of the neighborhood council charged with disbursing the money.

Some arrangement would have to be made for protecting the tenants against excessive rents after rehabilitation. The work itself, funded by public monies, could be one incentive to the landlord to accept a ceiling; further, the city could guarantee that the tax assessment would not be increased as long as the rents were not increased. Neighborhood residents could function as code enforcement officers, with or without portfolio, so that recalcitrant landlords would know that violations were not going unnoticed. City hall, often reluctant to enforce codes vigorously for fear of building abandonment, would be more willing to do so if funds for rehabilitation were at hand.

Citizen participation would be more than an administrative appendage of the program. City hall's role would be to establish neighborhood boundaries, see to the formation of neighborhood councils, apportion the money among them—then let them decide how to spend it. In white neighborhoods, this could be a stimulus to organize for positive, rather than defensive, purposes. In black neighborhoods, it would have the effect of placing tools in the hands of those who now, without resources, can only express their pride through aggression. It also would open new employment opportunities: The skills that go into minor rehabilitation, for example, are easily learned; the work is not held so tightly in the hands of craft unions as new construction.

Such a program would keep many more housing units in the market than could be built—or rehabilitated to present standards—with the same money. It would not substitute for permanent improvement of the neighborhood and its housing, any more than it would solve a city's revenue problems. But it would be a tangible beginning, a holding action to prevent further deterioration while larger programs are being planned and mounted.

2. *The creation of additional community-service jobs.* The condition of the urban environment reflects a basic fact of contemporary American life: The public sector is not getting its work done. The private sector of American endeavor each year rises to new heights of productivity and accomplishment; the public sector each year adds to the accumulation of tasks untended. Individually we keep our house in order. As a community, as a society, we are careless, neglectful, continually putting off until tomorrow what should have been done long before today.

The fact is most readily apparent in the shoddy physical condition of the city, the inadequacy of public transportation systems, the build-up of pollution in the air and waterways. But it applies equally to health, and especially to mental health; to education; to social services; to law enforcement; to every area in which human concern touches public responsibilities. Experts in any one of these areas could present the nation with a long agenda of unfinished business.

The irony is that, with all this work to be done, millions are out of jobs. More millions work, but sporadically and for a wage that leaves them poor. Some—no one knows quite how many—have stopped trying, are out of the labor force entirely. All this at a time of unprecedented prosperity.

The linkage between these two phenomena—the unmet public agenda, the seemingly impervious pockets of poverty and unemployment at a time of plenty—has been identified by almost every serious student of either. The National Commission on Technology, Automation, and Economic Progress estimated, in 1966, that as many as 5.3 million public-service jobs could be created without resort to make-work activities. The Urban Coalition, in 1967, called for the immediate creation of a million such jobs through federal assistance as the

fastest, most efficient means of easing the restless poverty of
the slums and ghettos. The Civil Disorders Commission, in
1968, also adopted the million-job goal, to be met over a
three-year period and with emphasis on "employing trainees
to improve rundown neighborhoods and to perform a variety
of other socially useful public services."

The creation of new community-service jobs with built-in
training programs, then, is another logical starting point. First
among the reasons is the crucial role that the dearth of jobs
plays in making the slum-ghettos what they are. Employment,
Moynihan was quoted as saying in the Civil Disorders Commission report, "is the primary source of individual or group
identity. In America, what you do is what you are: To do
nothing is to be nothing; to do little is to be little. The equations are implacable and blunt, and ruthlessly public."

A historically small number of Americans today are unable
to find something to do. In the fourth quarter of 1968, unemployment in the nation's large metropolitan areas (250,000
population or more) was down to 3.2 per cent. But there remained some gaps. For whites the rate was 2.8 per cent and
for Negroes, 6.1 per cent. In the "poverty areas" of the nation's hundred largest cities—the fifth of the census tracts that,
in 1960, ranked lowest on an index of income, education,
skills, housing, and family stability—the Negro unemployment
rate was 9 per cent. Normally, an over-all rate of 6 per cent
signifies recession. Thus, while whites were enjoying the employment benefits of unprecedented prosperity, blacks were in
a recession—and the slums and ghettos had not even reached
that level. Among black teenagers in such neighborhoods,
27.3 per cent were unemployed.

A word here about progress: The 6.1 per cent of the blacks
who were out of work in late 1968 represented the lowest percentage in five years for the large metropolitan areas. The
27.3 per cent unemployment rate for black teenagers in poverty areas was down sharply from the 34 per cent recorded in
the last quarter of 1967. But both these signs of progress must

be considered in the context of a booming economy. The Council of Economic Advisers was stating a truism when it said, in 1969: "The hard-core unemployed, the educationally disadvantaged, and the victims of discrimination are the last to be hired during a return to high employment and the first to be fired during a slowdown." A few months of general recession in 1954, the CEA pointed out, had wiped out four years of gain. Sure enough, figures for the first quarter of 1969, when the Administration's inflation warriors were complaining that the economy had not slowed enough, showed a .9 per cent rise in the over-all rate of black unemployment. There was no guarantee that this was the start of a trend, but it was a reminder of how fragile black progress can be.

Even if the economy continued at present speed, the council said, its impact on the hard-core unemployed would gradually diminish. The reason is to be found in the Labor Department's ten-city survey of 1966, which pointed out that employment problems in the slum-ghettos often were "matters of *personal* rather than *economic* conditions."[2] The survey report took pains to say it did not mean that the slum-ghetto resident lacked the incentive to work: 80 per cent of the unemployed polled in the survey said they would welcome the chance for on-the-job training; in Philadelphia, one of the ten cities, a training program had a waiting list of 6,000; in Oakland, a "Job Fair" attracted 15,000 persons—and placed 250. By personal conditions it meant inferior education (a third of the unemployed adults in the ten slum-ghettos had never attended high school), health problems (in an Oakland "Skill Center," 40 per cent of the trainees were found to be held back by a need for eyeglasses), police records, or past wage garnishments because of bad debts. The large number of households headed by women—37 per cent of all households in the ten slum-ghettos—meant that lack of child care was a significant factor in the unemployment rate.

At the time of the survey, unemployment in these ten areas stood at 9.3 per cent (the national rate was then 3.5 per cent).

But that was by no means the full extent of the employment gap. It was this survey that first focused on the significance of *sub*employment in the slums and ghettos. Adding the unemployed to those working part time not by choice and those working full time but still in poverty, the Labor Department found that a third of the residents in the survey areas had serious job problems.

Taking a further step, the Civil Disorders Commission placed its emphasis on the quality as well as the number of jobs available to slum-ghetto residents. Black workers, it said,

> are concentrated in the lowest skilled and lowest paying occupations. These jobs often involve substandard wages, great instability and uncertainty of tenure, extremely low status in the eyes of both employer and employee, little or no chance for meaningful advancement, and unpleasant or exhausting duties. Negro men in particular are more than three times as likely as whites to be in unskilled or service jobs which pay far less than most.

The commission offered a detailed Census Bureau breakdown for the year 1966 to prove the point. *One Year Later*, a privately sponsored report assessing progress since the commission issued its findings, updated the figures to 1968—and found virtually no change in the pattern.

This concentration at the lowest end of the scale of employment status and rewards, the commission said, "is the single most important source of poverty among Negroes." It has other effects as well. In areas where almost the only work available to blacks is menial work, there is a lower proportion of blacks than whites in the labor force—the blacks saying, in effect, "Why try?" In areas where there are more skilled and semiskilled jobs open to blacks, they are represented in the labor force in roughly the same proportion as whites.

Further, the kinds of jobs most often available to blacks don't pay enough to support a family and, in the commission's words, "lack the necessary status to sustain a worker's self-

respect, or the respect of his family or friends." Wives are
forced to work (and often earn more money than their husbands), tensions arise at home, and the husband leaves. The
most depressing current statistic about urban life relates to the
number of fatherless homes. Between 1959 and 1967, the percentage of Negro families in the cities headed by a female rose
from 23 to 30. The welfare system, of course, has made its
contribution to this increase by the denial, in many states, of
assistance to families where there was a father who earned
something, though not enough to support his children. In
such a situation, the father could do better by his family if he
moved out and let them get welfare payments.

Education, the commission suggested, doesn't make that
much difference in the kind of job the slum-ghetto resident
can get—a fact that is not lost on black teenagers. It was sub-
stantiated, in early 1969, by a voluminous report of the Equal
Employment Opportunity Commission (EEOC) based on a
1966 survey of 43,000 companies.[3] EEOC sifted the survey
data two ways, and found that the lower educational level
of minorities "accounts for only about one-third of the difference in occupational ranking between Negro men and ma-
jority-group men. The inevitable conclusion is that the other
two-thirds must be attributed to discrimination, deliberate or
inadvertent."

What this means was described to a congressional committee by sociologist Elliot Liebow, who lived for a while in a
Washington, D.C. ghetto with those he called "the street-
corner men." The young black looks around and finds that
what he can look forward to, in the way of a career, is to become a busboy or a dishwasher. If he tries hard in school, he
can become an educated busboy or dishwasher. And if he
applies himself diligently to his work, he can become an educated, hard-working busboy or dishwasher. That is what the
statistics mean. That is what is called a future in the slums
and ghettos.

If there is a core problem in these neighborhoods—one aspect of life here that, more than any other, breeds alienation, breeds resentment, breeds corollary problems of violence and social disorganization—this it is. This is the handle that, if turned, could make maximum immediate difference. There is widespread agreement on this conclusion and on the proposition that the provision of jobs is a task to be shared by the public and private sectors. But so far the response has come mainly from the private side.

Heartening as this response is, there is reason to question whether it can be sufficient to the need—whether, in fact, private industry has been asked to assume the right portion of the task. The companies involved in the National Alliance of Businessmen and like efforts to employ the hard core are, by their own acknowledgment, finding the job enormously difficult. It strains the capacity and sympathy of supervisors, particularly at the middle level and below, and involves them in all manner of activities foreign to the world of sound business practice. It is so difficult that manpower experts Samuel M. Burt and Herbert E. Striner of the Upjohn Institute, a nonprofit research organization specializing in manpower policy, suggested, in the fall of 1968, that only the largest of companies could be expected to try.[4] Even large companies, Burt and Striner said, are approaching this particular form of public service on an experimental basis and may not stay with it indefinitely. "Don't ask the employer to turn his plant and office into a social service agency or an educational institution," they admonished. This is not, and will not become, the business of business on any scale large enough to make a difference. Their proposed alternative is, essentially, to make every agency of government a training agency. Government should provide, and is not now providing, the same kind of entry-level opportunities for the hard core that it is currently asking of private industry. Government agencies should be given the same kind of financial aid now offered private industry to make the effort. They should assume responsibility for teaching the hard-core recruit how to do a job—and how to keep one; for preparing him to move on, either into the civil service or into private firms. Burt and Striner specifically reject the widely advocated concept of "government as employer of last resort," providing jobs if all else fails. Instead, they propose that government be the "employer of initial employment opportunity."

Government's role would then be twofold: to give the disadvantaged "salable skills for which industry will be glad to compete"; and to create, within government, "new careers—subprofessional trainee types of jobs in areas of government service, desperately needed but not yet offered because of lack of funds." Upjohn conducted a survey of opportunities for development of these new public-service careers in large cities. It found them plentiful, in areas ranging from antipollution enforcement to recreation. It found also that the need for services was great enough, in itself, to be "the underlying justification for public-service employment."

There are two further facets of the problem that support this approach. One is geography; the fact is, the hard-core unemployed live far from where private enterprise is building new jobs. Given all the will (and capacity) in the world on the part of private enterprise, there would remain the problem of getting the jobless out to where the jobs are. The hard-core unemployed now live in the heart of those areas most in need of expanded public services.

The second aspect springs from pride and the natural desire of man to control his own destiny. A public-service employment program, beyond providing jobs and services, could fulfill this need. Involving the residents of the slums and ghettos in the delivery of public services could be the means of involving them actively in the day-to-day operations of government.

Consider, for a single example, the matter of the schools. In the last year or two, the schools have been the center of a civic action that began with demands for citizen participation and has escalated to demands for community control. The debate over the merits of integration versus ghetto-school enrichment has been subsumed by this new surge. Even blacks who remain "moderate" in their views have, if they are parents, become involved in, and activated by, the community-control movement, and it is spreading from city to city.

The reasons are not hard to determine. Every parent has some concern over the delegation of his authority to an institution. Imagine the intensification of concern if the school, year after year, returns children damaged, further behind society's standards and demands than when they started. This is what, by every measure, slum-ghetto schools have been doing. The blame is not exclusively theirs—it is shared by society—but that has been the performance record.

Seeing no hope of escape, watching the present proprietors do so badly, the slum-ghetto residents are asking for a chance to try their hand at improving the situation. They are proposing that the children might respond better to adults more like themselves, adults who understand their problems because they share them. The goals are not extravagant, even though the means may be abrasive. Still, the degree and form of community involvement in the schools is proving exceedingly difficult to work out. The attempt to do so in New York split that city and increased its tensions as much as any recent event—and the end of conflict is far from sight.

One partial, temporary form of school-community linkage suggested by the Civil Disorders Commission was maximum use of residents, especially parents, as teachers' aides and in other paraprofessional roles. There is a real need in ghetto schools for more adults—to increase individual instruction or simply to keep discipline while teaching goes on. Theirs could be a friendly presence, diminishing the impersonality of the classrooms and hallways, linking the experience of home and school.

A public-service employment program could put these people in the schools, not just to improve their children's attitudes and achievements, but to increase and expand their own

learning. They could be given special training linked to opportunities to enter the school system with professional status.
Such a program would not end the community-control con-
flicts, which involve that most precious of commodities,
power. But it would be another holding action and, in the
meantime, might establish linkages and contacts that would
make resolution of the larger issue easier. It might also ease
the damage to the current generation of children.

Beyond employment programs, there are two other means
of black economic advancement that have been widely discussed. One is Mr. Nixon's black capitalism, since renamed
"minority entrepreneurship." At present, blacks own and operate less than 1 per cent of the nearly 5 million private businesses in the nation. Fewer than 3 per cent of the 1.5 million
Americans who classify themselves as self-employed are black.
Most of them run small, marginal enterprises serving a market
characterized largely by low purchasing power. In a nation
whose major business remains business, there is no part of
the system in which exclusion of blacks is more complete.

Concern with this exclusion mounted during 1968 as it
became clear that the major targets of civil disorders were
white-owned shops and stores in the ghettos. The remedies
proposed have fallen into two categories: economic development of the ghetto, and aid to individual blacks to enter business without regard to where. Public and private efforts
toward both ends have increased greatly. The Small Business
Administration has turned its attention from Main Street to
the cities and, in fourth quarter 1968, increased the number of loans to minorities by more than 200 per cent and the
amount of such loans by nearly 300 per cent, over the same
period of 1967. (There has since been some retrenchment by
the new Administration.) Private firms and organizations such
as the American Bankers Association and the Menswear Re-
tailers of America have launched major assistance programs,
and Negro-aid groups, including the giant Urban League, have
made entrepreneurship a major focus of their activities.

The emphasis is justified, if only to end the awful symbolism of this particular form of black dependency. But it is employment, not entrepreneurship, that offers hope of immediate and large-scale help to the black poor. A 2 per cent increase in salaries and wages of black workers, economist Sar A. Levitan has pointed out, would do more to ease black poverty than a 100 per cent increase in black business profits, even assuming blacks shared with proportional equality in business ownership. Black business development, moreover, normally does not involve the poor: Howard Samuels, who headed the Small Business Administration during its time of reorientation, frankly acknowledged that the objective was "not to put the poor in business but to put the minorities in business." Finally, putting the minorities in business is turning out to be a painstaking, one-at-a-time task, and it will be years before it makes a noticeable impact. "We seize on a few glowing examples and imply somehow that it has made a difference," said Andrew Bennett of the Economic Development Administration's Urban Projects Division in early 1969. "But we're talking about 25 million people. There's just not enough being invested to bring about change."

Black capitalism, then, is worth encouraging for its own sake and its own objectives, but not as a substitute for a major push for employment. The same can be said of the second alternative route to economic progress, a government guarantee of minimum income. This, too, is an idea that has risen rapidly in academic and government circles. President Nixon, in the "family-assistance system" with which he hopes to replace welfare, has proposed to put a $1,600 floor under family income (although denying, with more passion than logic, it would be an income guarantee).

The income-maintenance idea comes in several forms: a negative-income tax, which would pay families part of the difference between what they make and the poverty line; a guaranteed annual income, which would make up the entire poverty gap; a family allowance—a form of income supplement now in effect in every major industrial democracy except our own. Common to all is the concept that the defining characteristic of the poor is their lack of money. The nation takes enormous administrative pains, proponents argue, to give money to the poor indirectly through welfare payments, housing subsidies, school lunch programs, veterans' benefits, unemployment compensation, old-age and disability payments, and so on down the list. Many of the poor fall between the categories—only about a third receive public assistance—and others are harrassed by complex rules and rigorous administrators fearful of waste. Wouldn't it be simpler just to give them money as their right?

Paul Douglas, the economist and former U.S. Senator, is a dissenter from this argument. He believes income-maintenance plans would be expensive, would not materially reduce the need for administrative scrutiny, and would not substitute for all the services provided by the welfare system (which he readily admits is in need of drastic reform). Douglas also feels that the American people are far from accepting the idea: "They are afraid," he says, "that most men are as lazy as they dare to be." Substantiation for his view of public opinion came in a Gallup poll of June, 1968. Two propositions were presented to the respondents: that government should guarantee every American a job, and that government put a floor under every American's income. Guaranteed employment was supported by 78 per cent of the respondents and guaranteed income by only 36 per cent.

The two are not mutually exclusive. They could be combined in a strategy of providing jobs for all who can work and providing a minimum income, by the simplest and most direct possible means, to those who cannot work. The vast majority of slum-ghetto residents want to make their own way, dislike dependency. To make it pridefully, they need more than money. They need jobs. And again, the means of providing jobs could be a public-service employment program that also gets at the nation's unfinished public business.

The program has thus far been described in terms of the job and income problems of slum-ghetto residents because they most painfully, most resentfully feel economic want. But the guaranteed-job–guaranteed-income strategy would apply to all, as a matter of individual right and national conscience. Further, the creation of new jobs in public service could ease black-white tensions by reducing the tragic competition for pieces of an employment pie that is, at present, too small to go quite all the way around. Increasing training opportunities without increasing the total number of jobs, conversely, can worsen these tensions.

Would this program worsen Mr. Nixon's domestic priority problem, inflation? Perhaps, if countervailing measures were not taken. The point to be made here, without extensive economic discussion, is that there must be ways to fight inflation that do not require the poor to pay the price.

3. *The restoration of law and order in the cities.* Fear is the greatest single contributor to the tense division of the cities and society. The generators of fear, as was noted earlier, have included the assassinations, civil disorders, street protests, and campus strife at both high school and college levels. But what keeps fear alive daily in the cities is crime in the streets. Until crime subsides, is stopped in its epidemic spread, there will be no end to fear—and, thus, little hope of progress. A reduction of crime and violence must therefore be a starting point toward making the nation one.

The words "law and order" are used deliberately in describing this task because they are badly in need of rescue. They were used loosely and irresponsibly in the year 1968, thus contributing to the spread of fear. The orators of law and order were unable or unwilling to make some essential distinctions: between the rule of law and the imposition of order, between crime and mass violence, among kinds of crime and kinds of violence, between what the enforcers of law can do and what society at large must do. Perhaps the largest of all these neglected distinctions was the one between "tolerating" crime and violence and understanding the anatomy and causes of crime and violence so these could be dealt with precisely, rationally, and democratically.

When the orators, for example, raged (sometimes violently) against violence and lawlessness, they clearly lumped civil disorders in the same category as street crime. Now there are certain points of commonality between violent crime and civil disorders: Both do involve the breaking of laws; both mainly occur in, and mainly damage, the slums and ghettos; both have a dual cause-effect relationship to the social disorganization found there. Yet the differences between crime and civil disorders are more significant: Crime often is planned and almost always undertaken for private motives such as profit, rage, or revenge; civil disorders have been notably spontaneous and communal, carried on by large numbers of people moved to protest.

These differences have important implications. They indicate that the remedies for civil disorders are to be found in the causes of protest, which take up much of this book. There are not many significant measures that could be labelled "civil-disorder prevention" and put in the manuals of law enforcement agencies (although there is much these agencies could do, as shall be seen, to avoid being among the causes of civil disorders). The task of prevention is more properly assigned to society at large.

The distinctive nature of civil disorder, as opposed to crime, also implies a different form of immediate response. Protest must be handled with care in a democracy, a form of government that is defined in part by the right of protest. When protest takes a form that breaks the law, the law-breaking must be stopped—but in a way that does least damage to a social fabric already rended. That was the significance of the new form of response first introduced in the civil disorders of April, 1968, which placed emphasis on a show of massive force and on mass arrests rather than on the bloody, bullet-marked counterviolence with which police and National Guardsmen responded in summer of 1967. The change was proposed by the Civil Disorders Commission, devised by the Justice Department under Attorney General Ramsey Clark, and introduced at a series of winter seminars co-sponsored by the International Association of Chiefs of Police. All deserve the nation's gratitude: While the number of civil disorders increased nearly 200 per cent in 1968, the number of deaths decreased from 84 to 69. Despite the ragings of Richard Daley, the new system did not, as he seemed to suggest, leave the cities defenseless. It simply substituted arrests for killings.

Crime also has its roots in other forms of social distress—poverty, idleness, family instability—and would be reduced if they were eased. In the meantime, however, there are a great many specifics to the task of crime prevention and control that are susceptible to change. For the day-to-day performance of this task, society relies on the specialists who comprise the criminal-justice system: law enforcement agencies, the courts, and correctional institutions. The rise in crime reflects the nation's general social malaise, but it also reflects the fact that the criminal-justice system is in a condition of serious malfunction. Immediate reform of the system could do much to control crime while the slower process of social reform continues.

It could begin with the police, who are society's first line of defense on the streets—and who are, all too literally, on the firing line. "Every policeman in this country carries at his hip a machine that can blow almost any incident in the ghetto into a full-scale riot," Howard Leary, New York City's Police Commissioner, testified to the Civil Disorders Commission in 1967. Feared, even hated, often goaded beyond normal limits of restraint, in daily contact with the worst elements of the neighborhood, the police carry all of the burdens of society and history into the streets of the slum-ghetto.

Their problems and performance were examined in detail by a task force of the President's Crime Commission, which delivered a landmark ten-volume report in 1967.[5] The police, the task force made clear, are neither well chosen, well trained, nor well paid for their terrible responsibilities. "Existing selection requirements and procedures in the majority of departments, aside from physical requirements, do not screen out the unfit," said the task force. "Hence, it is not surprising that many of those charged with protecting life and property and rationally enforcing our laws are not respected by their fellow officers and are incompetent, corrupt, or abusive." The task force cited a survey of 300 police departments that showed 24 per cent had no minimal educational requirements and only 1 per cent required college training (of 22 departments that do, 21 were in California). Although most required a high-school diploma, there were many that did not even go that far. Yet the police, by testimony of Quinn Tamm, executive director of the International Association of Chiefs of Police, "engage in the difficult, complex, and important business of human behavior. Their intellectual armament—so long restricted to the minimum—must be no less than their physical prowess."

Society shows its respect for various occupations by how it pays them. In 1960, the task force said, the median salary for professional and technical workers was $7,124; for craftsmen and foremen $5,699; and for police $5,321. To attract college-trained recruits, the task force estimated that starting salaries would have to be $7,000 to $10,000 (at 1967 wage levels), with a maximum of $15,000 after long service. Police departments at present pay nowhere near these kinds of salaries and therefore have trouble attracting anyone at all. The 300-department survey showed that 65 per cent of the forces were below authorized strength, those in big cities by an average of 10 per cent. They have special problems attracting Negroes, which many are now trying to do. One reason may be found in task force figures on promotions: Whites entering northern police departments have a 1-in-8 chance of becoming sergeants and a 1-in-45 chance of becoming captains. The corresponding figures for blacks are 1-in-20 and 1-in 311.

The task force found police training to be generally inadequate in every area but one, where it was "woefully inadequate." That area was police-community relations. The task force surveyed 165 police departments in large cities and smaller cities that had significant minority populations. In 22, there was no community-relations training at all; in the others, it averaged a total of 11 hours. The task force said that 120 hours would be desirable and 60 a minimum.

Society, then, is not sending its best men out to be its most visible agents on the street, and those it is sending out are poorly prepared to understand the problems they will find there. But it is more serious than that. Attitudes within the police department ensure that the ghetto streets will get the poorest of an unprofessional lot. Assignments to the ghetto, the task force said, are given "as punishment, a kind of exile." Albert Reiss, director of the Center for Research on Social Organization at the University of Michigan, told the Civil Disorders Commission, "The slum police precinct is like the slum school. It gets, with few exceptions, the worst in the system." By worst Reiss meant, in part, the most prejudiced. Reiss reported on extensive research he had done in the police department of an unidentified city. He found only 1 per cent of the police in the city's slum precincts in any way sympathetic to Negroes, and nearly half extremely prejudiced against them. By extreme prejudice, Reiss said, he meant that the slum police spoke of Negroes "in terms of the animal kingdom."

The street gets the message. The police aren't there to protect them, much less to help them, but to keep them in line. "Looking at the police from the point of view of a Negro," says Bayard Rustin, "you have to think of the police as jailers. If you have a ghetto, which is like a jail, in which people are kept, they end up looking upon the policeman ultimately as responsible for keeping them there."

Police brutality is a frequent complaint in the ghetto. In the UCLA study, most of the Watts-area residents held the belief that police were more violent than they needed to be. Questioned about police abuse—brutality plus "insulting comments, rousting or frisking of individuals unnecessarily, and stopping or searching cars without cause"—a third of the male Negro respondents said they had experienced these things and half said they had seen them happen. Neither the Crime Commission nor the Civil Disorders Commission attempted any measurement of police brutality; neither questioned its existence.

But lack of police protection is a more frequent complaint. The Crime Commission found that while one out of every two whites believes the police provide "very good" protection in his neighborhood, only one Negro in five does. The Civil Disorders Commission speaks of a "dual standard of law enforcement." It cites a *Yale Law Journal* study of Hartford that found that, while residents of the central Negro ghetto were victims of about a third of the daylight burglaries in the city, only one of the city's eighteen patrol cars and one of its eleven foot patrolmen were assigned there. The U.S. Civil Rights Commission once monitored police communications records in Cleveland. The records showed that it took four times as long to respond to robbery calls in a Negro district as in the white district where response was next slowest.

The police do not cause crime in the ghetto, but their practices contribute to it. To the extent that there is selective enforcement of law, the ghetto becomes a haven for those who want to escape the law. In particular, it becomes a haven for the narcotics peddlers, who spread habits beyond the means of their victims to support and thus generate a large proportion of street robberies. Lack of police protection breeds fear in the street, and fear contributes to the social disorganization that inevitably breeds crime. Police abuse diminishes respect for the law, and thus weakens the social controls that can, more effectively than any nightstick, reduce crime.

Once again, it should be recognized that the policeman's lot is not an easy one, particularly in the distressed and hostile atmosphere of the slums and ghettos. Nor is it made any easier by the condition of the other parts of the criminal-justice system, the courts and correctional institutions. James Q. Wilson, a political scientist who recently has been special-izing in the study of crime, has suggested that reform of these elements of the system, even more neglected than police re-form, may offer the prospect of an especially high payoff.[6] Wilson's thesis is based on the fact that nearly 90 per cent of those arrested each year have previous records. The courts and correctional institutions, in other words, already have had their chance with these repeaters and have failed.

The courts, for their part, are simply inundated. At the time the Crime Commission report was written, trial delay averaged eight and a half months. By the end of 1968, it had stretched to ten months. One result, especially discouraging to police, is that many of those they arrest walk the streets for these months, free to try again. (Paradoxically, these are likely to be the most serious criminals, who can afford bail; the poor simply stay in jail, awaiting their turn at "justice.") Many others escape full punishment because the crowded courts, in self-defense, accept shortcut procedures—such as guilty pleas to lesser offenses—to avoid time-consuming, full-scale trials. Wilson reports a 1964 California survey of 18,746 robberies, roughly 10,000 of which resulted in arrests. Of those arrested, he says,

> over 40 per cent were released by the police without charges; felony complaints were filed against only one-third. Of these, about a fifth had the complaints dismissed at a preliminary hearing; of these, about a tenth were dismissed at arraignment and another 8 per cent were acquitted after a trial. Of the 1,600 persons pleading or found to be guilty, 82 per cent went to jail or prison. Thus, of the 10,000 persons arrested, only 13 per cent were incarcerated.

The suspicion is that, were the courts operating with greater efficiency, the percentage would have been higher.

Beyond efficiency, there is also a suspicion that a court system so overburdened may be delivering something less than justice. The New Jersey Select Commission on Civil Disorder did a detailed study of Part I of Newark's Municipal Court. Part I deals with disorderly conduct and other misdemeanors frequent on the street. This is how the commission described Part I's operation, from arrest to disposition of a case:

After arrest, the defendant is taken to the precinct house where he can post bail. Usually, in Part I, bail ranges from $100 to $2,500, depending on the nature of the charge and the nature of the defendant. A bondsman charges a fee of at least 10 per cent and often requires collateral. Therefore, the poor usually go on to the police department's central cell block to await trial and, on the average, remain there overnight or over a weekend. The cells there are about 5-by-8 feet and have no lights. The cell block has been condemned by the State Department of Institutions and Agencies.

If the case is not disposed of on the defendant's appearance before the magistrate of Part I, he goes to Essex County Jail where he spends, on the average, two weeks. The county jail was designed for 308 prisoners but, at the time of the commission study, had 433. The defendant is not likely to hire a lawyer or prepare a defense if it means a longer stay in the county jail. He cannot telephone a lawyer and his letters are censored.

When his trial comes up, the defendant goes on what the chief magistrate of Newark's municipal courts himself has described as an "assembly line." The time of the trial is typically two to twelve minutes. The defendant is told of his rights but, as the commission says, "whether defendants understand what they are told is a different question. The time available offers little opportunity and the atmosphere little encouragement to bring up questions." Less than half of the defendants (40 per cent according to the chief magistrate, 23 per cent according to the commission) are represented by lawyers. The public defender's office does not get involved in the minor crimes that come before Part I. Private lawyers who take Part I cases complain of being treated, in the words of one to the commission, "like obstructionists."

Those who go through the punishing process described above do so before they are convicted of any crime: They are sentenced to it merely by arrest and poverty. The ones who are formally convicted pass into the next part of the criminal-justice system, corrections, which may be the most overburdened and most neglected part of all. "All too often," Wilson has said, "the choice in many states is between locking a person up in an overcrowded prison or assigning him to an overworked probation officer. In prison he does time and little else; when he's on probation nobody knows what he does."

The result is the high rate of recidivism. Instead of correcting, the prisons become incubators of criminal careers. Wilson proposes "a range of correctional alternatives suitable for different perpetrators with different prospects of correction." The Crime Commission described a California experiment in which prisoners went out to work or to attend school during the days and returned on nights and weekends; their rate of recidivism was 28 per cent in comparison with the 52 per cent rate of recidivism of a "control group" of conveniently locked-up prisoners.

Replication of such experiments is prevented by public indifference—corrections, the Crime Commission said, is the part of the system "that the public sees least of and knows least about"—and by ideology. Correctional programs, Wilson says, are regarded by the public as either "tough" or "soft"; the prisoner is either "abused" or "mollycoddled." There is no middle ground, no pragmatic testing of how the programs might be working out. The result, he continues, is that "almost any proposal to improve the correctional element of the system is opposed by liberals if it seems to involve expanding conventional prison facilities and opposed by conservatives if it seems to provide nonprison alternatives."

The same ideological hang-ups inhibit reform of the criminal-justice system as a whole. Until recently, any attention paid to crime was considered an illiberal diversion from the social problems that cause crime. Hence, the field was left to reactionaries—and they have made the most of it. To them, the problem is society's "permissiveness," bred of a crime-coddling conspiracy to weaken the nation's moral fiber, a conspiracy that has included the Supreme Court, Dr. Spock, and, almost certainly, the Communist enemy. What it comes down to is that you are either for the police or against them. So far, argues this group, the police have been shackled by the courts and politicians; it's time to take the shackles off.

Given the current level of public fear, this line has proved persuasive in virtually every recent electoral test. Law and order, and particularly the role of the police, has become the most powerful political issue of the day. It carries a deep and fundamental danger to our political system. Already, sensing their power, the police are acting with noticeably less restraint—in Chicago, in Berkeley, in Oakland, in New York (where, not too long ago, off-duty officers attacked a handful of Black Panthers in a Brooklyn courthouse hallway). They are showing signs of an our-side, their-side mentality—"their side" being, interchangeably, the blacks and the long-haired kids—which could make the police less peace officers than the advance guard of race and class warfare.

The most genuine threat to this country in the year 1969 is not that the blacks will burn the cities down, nor that the young will tear the schools and colleges apart. These things can and will be prevented. Rather, it is the threat that, in fear and revulsion, we will slide toward totalitarianism. Another term for totalitarianism is the police state.

The police must never be given impunity in deciding who is to be punished, and how, and for what. The police have the right to defend themselves and to halt anyone running from the scene of a felony, but even this authority must be used with the greatest restraint in a situation as tense as today's. If this restraint is not inbred, then it must be imposed.

The police are not a power apart in our society, with some

special mandate to wreak vengeance on wrongdoers. They are an agency of local government with an especially difficult and demanding job to do, under "political"—which is to say social and governmental—control just like any other agency. If the police don't like politics they should stay out of it, and if any policeman does not see himself as an arm and agent of government, he should get off the force. Anyone who advocates "unleashing" the police in the present situation is advocating the first step toward abandoning democracy.

The cities need stronger police forces, which is to say better, rather than harsher, police forces. This means, as the Civil Disorders and Crime Commissions have both pointed out, better pay, better training, and higher standards of admission. The racists should be screened and weeded out; the rest of the force taught more about the problems of the street; the best, rather than the worst, put in the most sensitive situations. (The Civil Disorders Commission suggests special "combat pay" for those in the ghetto.) The department should be tied more closely to the general community: The Crime Commission proposed, and the Civil Disorders Commission seconded the idea, that the force include "community-service officers" recruited from the neighborhood as a link between the precinct and the street. Both commissions called for better grievance mechanisms so that the police do not act as judge and jury in cases of alleged police misconduct.

Similarly, the cities need more and better—not sterner— judges, so that justice returns to courtrooms that have come to resemble automated factories; better means of correction, so that the same faces do not show up in the courts and precinct houses again and again. They need, in sum, a restoration of the rule of law, justly and competently applied, from which order can follow. Peace, and full justice, will come only from far-reaching political, social, and economic change. But specific and immediate reform of the criminal-justice system can restore an atmosphere in which peace and change can be pursued.

8

Building
Choice

The National Commission on Urban Problems, established by President Johnson in 1967 under the scholarly chairmanship of former Senator Paul Douglas, had as its fields of inquiry such undramatic topics as building codes, zoning, and property taxes. It subsequently broadened its study to include the entire process of urbanization. In June, 1968, the commission interrupted its quiet taking of testimony to drop a bombshell. It took the form of a projection of future population trends, which told a nation in trouble that, in effect, the nation hadn't seen anything yet.

The projection was the work of two leading demographers, Patricia Leavey Hodge and Philip M. Hauser, and it covered the period from 1960 to 1985.[1] By then, the figures indicated, there will be 178 million people living in the nation's metropolitan areas, compared to 113 million in 1960. They will represent 71 per cent of the total American population. Commission chairman Douglas suggested, in the foreword to the report, that it was time public officials began considering with some seriousness how they were going to provide the "housing, schools and city services" for 65 million more metropolitan residents.

According to the projection, the white population of the suburbs will more than double, increasing by 53.9 million; that of the central cities will decline by 2.4 million, or 5 per cent. The nonwhite population of the central cities will almost double, increasing by 10 million; that of the suburbs will increase, but only from 5 per cent of the total suburban population to 6 per cent. "The projections vividly portray the geographic fulfillment of the fears expressed by the President's Commission on Civil Disorders—that the American society is becoming an apartheid society," the authors commented.

Finally, an especially large increase was projected for three specific groups. The number of nonwhite elderly citizens in the cities will grow by 109 per cent. The number of nonwhite children under fifteen will grow by 92 per cent. And the number of young workers (ages fifteen to forty-four) among nonwhites will grow by 192 per cent. The demands for care, for schools, and for jobs that will be generated by the growth of these three groups were not projected.

The authors emphasized that their figures were projections, not predictions, which represent what present trends will produce—more separation, more young blacks out of school and out of work, larger ghettos—if present trends are allowed to continue. They need not, of course. There is nothing sacred about trends. There is nothing in the Constitution that says the nation cannot intervene in its own future.

This intervention, then, is the second essential element of a national urban policy, paralleling improvement in the lives of those who now live in the slums and ghettos. It involves taking a hand in the process called urbanization, in the deployment of land, of people, of jobs and economic activity as growth occurs. It also involves the task once described by President Johnson as the building of a "second America": the necessity to duplicate, by the end of this century, the nation's entire stock of physical facilities to meet this growth. In great part, the future will be shaped by how and where we build it, and for whom.

The motto by which we build at present is laissez-faire. The economic equations of the marketplace largely determine how and where urban development occurs. All but 20 per cent of the buildings added to the face of the nation each year are built by private enterprise for private purposes. Most of the subsidies by which we stimulate construction of housing for the poor and near-poor—less than 10 per cent of our annual housing production—go to private builders and financial institutions.

There is nothing sinister about all this: Private enterprise is the American way of building cities. Still, the public is remarkably permissive about how they are built. Most cities have shelves full of plans for the future—and only a handful of powers to see that the plans are carried out. Through subdivision ordinances they can decide when and in what sizes vacant property is to be put to residential use, but from that point on it is largely up to the builder. Through location of streets and utilities they can influence the direction of growth, but these decisions nearly always follow, rather than lead, the pull of the marketplace. Through zoning they can mandate the general uses of land and the size and placement of buildings, but zoning decisions are most frequently made through a tug of war between competing private interests. The public interest—our common stake in the quality of the urban environment—can get lost in the process. And the cities, of course, have no say at all about what is built beyond their boundaries.

Land in America is regarded not as a resource but as a commodity to be bought and developed or sold like any other. Land speculation is a major growth industry in which demand exceeds supply and prices therefore steadily rise. It is encouraged by the accepted way of taxing property, which is to assess development high and raw land low. The visible evidence of speculaton is the number of open parking lots on high-priced land in the center of cities: The owners accept a relatively low yield while they wait for values to rise still higher, "banking" their property beneath the cars.

Urban land, the Douglas Commission pointed out, is largely a manufactured item.[2] Its value is in great part created by the streets and transportation lines that make it accessible, the utilities that make it developable, the schools and other community facilities that make it attractive as a building site. These services and facilities, of course, are installed by public agencies. The profit resulting from the land's increased value goes into the pocket of the owner.

The result of this laissez-faire approach in metropolis is known as sprawl. Driven by rising land prices, builders go farther and farther out in their search of sites, often leap-frogging small, isolated parcels that stay vacant as scraggly remainders. Transportation and utility lines are stretched to the breakdown point, requiring constant, expensive extension. Arable land and open land that may some day be needed for recreation become increasingly hard to hold onto as development pressures push outward. Air becomes smudged and waterways smelly.

The city is left farther and farther behind. Those who leave it lose the benefits that only large concentrations of people can provide—cultural facilities, major sports and entertainment centers, hospitals offering the full range of medical knowledge. Those who stay live among private prosperity and public want. The great office towers continue to rise downtown, but what is not profitable is not built in cities pressed for revenue.

The laissez-faire approach to urban development works best for its proprietors. It works less well for the rest of us, who must make do with an environment built primarily for others' profit rather than for the satisfaction of our needs. It does not work at all for the poor and the minorities.

The problem for the poor is that they are outside the marketplace, yet subject to its laws. When money gets tight, not much finds its way into the mortgage-guarantee programs designed to build them shelter. When building costs go up, they collide with per-room spending ceilings for public housing, or FHA formulas that set maximum costs according to expected rentals. The resulting squeeze can stop these programs dead.

Rising land costs can have the same effect. The land is there, even in the largest cities: The Douglas Commission pointed out that 11 per cent of all the land parcels in Chicago were vacant lots. The figure for Los Angeles was 9.4 per cent; for New York, 8.1 per cent; even for Harlem, 2 per cent. More could be freed by tearing down vacant buildings, as the commission pointed out.

But two factors reduce the availability of land for low-income housing. One is its price, which, in the cities, forces housing agencies to build higher than they, or their clients, like. (Thus, the speculative portion of the marketplace takes its unearned toll.) The other factor, noted in an earlier chapter, has to do with the neighbors. George Schermer, a veteran consultant, wrote a depressing little history of the public housing program for the Douglas Commission, which shows how this factor works:[3]

Several states [in the program's early days] adopted laws requiring that all proposed public housing programs be subjected to referendum. In city after city the local authorities were forced to abandon vacant sites outside the central slum areas because of the objections of nearby white property owners. Racial fear and prejudice were at the root of much of the opposition, but there were other reasons for it. Public housing, by its very nature, meant large aggregations of the poor in settings reminiscent of the poor farm. Middle- and working-class people did not want this kind of intrusion into their neighborhoods. . . .

In many cities, compromises were made which led to debasement of the program. Often, the only sites available were in isolated, poorly developed "backwash" locations or on very expensive land in slum areas. Insofar as slum sites were used, land costs dictated the development of high-density, high-rise buildings.

The attack upon public housing at both the federal and local levels forced federal administrators and local authorities into a defensive position. The entire public housing bureaucracy was governed by the necessity of demonstrating to the critics that the housing being built was bare of any amenities which might be pleasing to the eye. Nothing suggesting comfort or "frills" could be included. It became a part of the creed that public housing was for shelter only.

The same creed applies to all programs for housing the poor.

In 1968, Congress adopted a new national housing goal calling for construction of 26 million units, 600,000 of them for low- and moderate-income families, in ten years. The numbers were drawn from two landmark studies: the Douglas Commission and the President's Committee on Housing. Both had independently arrived at similar estimates of housing need. Congress also added a variety of new wrinkles to the stock of federal programs: interest subsidies, public-housing variations to encourage private development and management, new sources of funds to guarantee mortgages, a partnership arrangement to draw in private investment. In all, the 1968 act was the most sweeping housing legislation since the years of the postwar building boom.

Its failure already is assured. Congress took the first steps toward seeing that the goals would not be met by denying full appropriations. But more significant was what Congress did not do. Nothing was written into the act that would put land under the subsidized housing units. The production of low-income housing is impeded by insufficient capital, which the act should help supply, and by inefficient building practices, which HUD Secretary George Romney, with an engaging faith in assembly lines, is trying to improve. But given all the money and technology the new goals require, they will not be met without unlocking the land. The key is a positive public role in land deployment and development, planned also to achieve the goal of a single society.

The Search for Sites

There are several alternative ways of seeking land for low-income housing. One is to concentrate the search in the slums and ghettos, where the most serious housing problems are.

HUD policies in this respect were conceived in, and have bred, what can only be called schizophrenia. With its right hand HUD, acting on the basis of civil rights laws and the Kennedy "stroke-of-a-pen" executive order banning segregation in federally aided housing, told the cities they could not concentrate low-income housing in the ghettos. With its left hand HUD aimed the urban-renewal and Model Cities programs squarely at the ghettos—and required that they emphasize construction of low-income housing.

In fairness, there is a cruel dilemma here that is not of HUD's making. Low-income housing is concentrated in the ghettos, as Schermer has shown, because other neighborhoods (including, in some cities, middle-class black neighborhoods) won't have it. Blacks and sympathetic mayors are torn between distaste for segregation and the crying need for housing, no matter where it has to be built. Federal policy is similarly torn, reflecting this dilemma, which is one reason for its current paralysis.

But even if all blacks began calling segregation separation and said "build here," and even if mayors and federal officials went along, there would remain formidable practical barriers to achieving the subsidized housing goals within the ghettos. Every year the housing agencies have proved anew how formidable these barriers are. New construction requires clearance, and no city has developed a program for relocation that is totally just or totally acceptable to the residents of the doomed dwellings. To talk clearance in many ghettos today is to light a tinder box. Nor have any but a few cities, in a few limited instances, devised a workable system for rehabilitation of housing in these historically blighted neighborhoods. If housing for the poor can be built only where the poor now live, and housing for blacks can be built only where blacks live, the housing goals will remain abstractions.

The second alternative is to say damn the neighbors and full speed ahead in the white and middle-income sectors of metropolis. These sectors have no right, in law or justice, to exclude blacks. Building in the white neighborhoods and sub-urbs would provide the relocation housing we need to clear the slums; it would also take away the sense of confinement that suffocates the ghettos. Even a few units at a time, on scattered sites, would help.

There is no disputing the justice or the logic of this argu-ment. But it must be pointed out once more that efforts to put low-income housing in "unpoor, unblack" neighborhoods have proved even more painful than ghetto improvement. Few mayors, in this day of militant white resistance, have the courage even to try within their cities. The suburbs, for their part, retain the legal means of keeping subsidized housing from their borders.

The nature of suburban resistance has been examined by Anthony Downs, of Real Estate Research Corporation, who identified three basic motives behind it:

> First, any influx of low-income households with children tends to add a net burden to local property taxes. Second, Americans who have "made it" into the middle class have traditionally sought to demonstrate their success by segregating themselves from those less affluent. This desire for relative economic and social homogeneity has important functions. It is much easier to pass on cherished values to one's children if they are reared in schools and neighborhoods where only children from fam-ilies with similar values are found. And personal security is much greater when one lives in an area where nearly all others accept the same standards of public deportment. . . . The third exclusionary motive is anti-Negro sentiment, which is still strong among many whites. It is reinforced by their falsely imputing lower-class traits to all Negroes and by their fears that Negro newcomers will depress property values.[4]

These are deep and powerful feelings, and they continue to face even those Negroes who make it through the suburbs' outer defenses. More are doing so: The number of Negroes moving into the suburbs annually increased from 20,000 be-fore 1966 to 220,000 in the years 1966–68. Still, there is little evidence that this rise represents progress. The aggregate difference between the incomes of blacks in the cities and in the suburbs is, by 1967 figures, about $10 per month. When the blacks get to the surburbs, moreover, they seldom find conditions any better there than in the city. What is happening is that the suburbs, especially the older ones closest to the city, are developing their own ghettos and their own slums. They are in the familiar cycle of slum creation: racial fear following the appearance of a few black families; flight of the whites; neglect of buildings by landlords as the neighborhood changes; overcrowding as decay sets in; and so on toward deterioration. If anything, the suburbs are less equipped, and less willing, to deal with this cycle than the more experienced cities.

More blacks than just the separatists are expressing reluctance to move into white neighborhoods. "There are many factors that restrain Negroes from responding to housing opportunities in suburban areas," said Schermer in a study of housing integration efforts for Potomac Institute, "not the least of which is the fact of life that discrimination is the rule and any other situation is the exception."[5] Schermer found that even in "open" developments the white customer was aggressively sold and the black customer merely accepted. Such developments are few and far between, and blacks can become understandably tired of knocking on locked doors, of moving from ghetto to ghetto—or of seeing a ghetto take shape around them, merely because of their presence.

None of this is meant to suggest that efforts to open new options to the poor and minorities should be abandoned. Such efforts are essential if we are to increase the low-income housing supply, improve the ghettos—and begin the process of ending social division before growth makes it permanent. "Residential segregation," the Civil Disorders Commission said, "prevents equal access to employment opportunities and obstructs efforts to achieve integrated education. A single society cannot be achieved as long as this cornerstone of segregation stands."

But it takes time to chip away a stone. Perhaps, in the interim, we can build around it.

The Scale of Concern

What is required to untie the present tangle is nothing less than an entirely new system of development. In outline, the system could work like this:

The federal government would redirect its development incentives to construction on the scale of communities, rather than individual housing units. Federal funds would be loaned to agencies at the state or local levels to acquire land. These agencies would plan new communities of 20,000 or more population, install improvements, set aside some sites for public facilities, then sell the rest for private development in accordance with the plan. As a condition of its land-acquisition loans, the federal government would require that a specified percentage of the housing units in the new communities be made available to low-income families. None of the housing would be designed for the poor, however: They would be given individual federal subsidies sufficient to pay the market price. Finally, the development agencies would repay the federal loans through profits from the resale of the land, so that the system would be self-replenishing.

Similar systems are operating successfully in Britain and other European countries, and have been for many years. It should be emphasized, however, that what is proposed here is not merely a new-towns program. The system could be used to create new towns and even new cities in virgin territory. But its greater utility would be inside or at the fringes of existing metropolitan areas. Advocates of new towns sometimes argue from the need to divert growth from metropolis before metropolis gets too big to be either livable or manageable. Yet even Great Britain, with the most extensive new-towns program of any democratic nation, has not succeeded in stemming the growth of the London area, the program's original purpose. Nor has Russia, with all its centralized state powers, been able to keep the population of Moscow stable, something it has been trying to do since the mid-1930's.

Like it or not, demographers agree that most of the 100 million additional Americans expected in the coming thirty-odd years will cluster in metropolis. Jerome Pickard, who did a set of detailed projections of the year 2000 population for the Urban Land Institute, has postulated that the bigger the metropolitan area of today, the larger will be its share of future growth. Perhaps some of it could be diverted to new towns or cities; the effort is worth making, if only to build examples, lacking now in America, of how satisfying a skillfully planned and designed urban environment can be. The larger need, however, is to find a way to *organize* the growth that inevitably will occur in metropolis, particularly at its expanding edges.

In particular, the need is to see that the growth of metropolis increases, rather than constricts, opportunities open to the poor and minorities. That is why the matter of scale is crucial to the development system outlined above. Pending massive changes in the minds and hearts of men, it will remain exceedingly difficult to introduce the poor and minorities into existing neighborhoods a few at a time. The effort to do so only exacerbates the fears and resentments of the working-class whites. It might be different in entirely new neighborhoods, desegregated from the start. The whites who moved into such neighborhoods likely would be younger, more pioneering in spirit and open in attitudes. They would know what they were moving into. Likewise, the minorities would not have the feeling they were invading somebody else's turf.

Schermer's Potomac Institute study of integrated housing showed that the larger the development, the larger the prospect that integration would succeed. The social goals of the new communities would be to open new options to the poor and minorities, to provide opportunities for contact between classes and races, and thus to lessen both confinement and division. But these goals do not require a perfect pepper-and-salt mix, building by building. Every street in the community would be open to all, but if blacks chose to live with blacks and whites with whites, nothing would or could be done about it. There would still be significant opportunities for contact on the communal scale—in the shopping centers, the theaters, the secondary schools.

Economic segregation within the new communities would be discouraged by ending the policy of building housing for the poor. There would be no large "projects" stigmatizing their occupants as second-level citizens. Instead, the poor would have access to the moderate-income units built by private developers—the majority of housing in the community —through rental or sales subsidies that made up the difference between the market price and a set percentage of their incomes.

The concept would be similar to the present rent-supplement program, but with one significant difference: Rent supplements are tied to construction of specific housing units for occupancy by the poor. Thus rent-supplement housing also carries a stigma. It is, moreover, built to the bleak standards Congress feels are appropriate to the poor. Like nearly all federal housing programs, rent supplements combine two objectives: to increase housing production and to shelter those in need.

There is a growing suspicion that these separate objectives require separate programs. The efforts to induce from the housing industry a few units for those with incomes below market level have been no less than tortuous and not notably productive. Perhaps the answer is to do as most European countries do: Increase the total housing output, as both presidential housing commissions said was necessary, with one form of subsidy. Make the poor the customers of the housing industry by giving them another form of subsidy, then let the industry do what it does best—serve a profitable market.

There is already in existence one major kind of housing allowance, as this form of subsidy is called, and that is the welfare check. It is not working very well. With the shortage of decent housing in the slums and ghettos, welfare recipients are forced to pay exorbitant rents, so their checks exert an inflationary influence on the housing market. The opponents of housing allowances warn that they could have a similar effect in any situation of scarcity.

But this would not be the situation in a new community. It would, in fact, offer an ideal testing ground for the housing allowance concept. Eventually, if the concept proved successful and enough new communities were built to ease the low-income housing shortage, the separation between subsidies to increase production and subsidies to shelter the poor could be made the rule in federal housing assistance. Certainly, if it did become the rule, it would ease the search for sites in existing cities and suburbs.

The leverage for applying this concept in the new communities would be federal land-purchase loans. The federal government might require, as one rule of thumb, that the percentage of housing units reserved for families receiving subsidies be no less than the percentage of low-income families in the nearest metropolitan area. (A similar yardstick was suggested by the Advisory Commission on Intergovernmental Relations in a landmark study of urban growth policy.[6]) The state or local development agency planning a new community would establish the economic mix of its housing, according to market projections, and offer land to private builders in parcels designated by housing price range. A condition of the sale of land for moderate-priced housing would be agreement by the builder to accept a specified number of subsidized families. The agency would be required to avoid concentrating the subsidy units in any one parcel.

What this means is that any family of modest means coming to the new community would have to accept the possibility of living next door to someone of lower economic status and perhaps another color. Given the deep class and race aversions described by Anthony Downs, would this tend to keep middle-class whites away?

The best hope that it would not—a genuine hope—is that prejudice often ends at the pocketbook. If the new community offered a bargain in terms of price, environment, and amenities, even nervous whites might be lured. Schermer found, in the Potomac study, that "persons who would prefer integration and those who would prefer segregation tend to place physical considerations and convenience ahead of their racial preferences."

This argues for a high standard of planning, design, and services in the new communities, the possibility of which, of course, is one reason for attempting to organize growth in the first place. Present random growth patterns create an economy of scarcity in public services and amenities. The choice of a place to live, for all but the wealthiest residents of metropolis, involves tradeoffs and compromises that can require the acceptance of daily inconvenience or worse.

We know how to do much better. The new town of Columbia, Maryland, is proving the fact. Its planning began, not with an "artist's conception" of a visionary environment, but with analysis of the kind of institutions the people of the town would need, performed by specialists in the areas of health, education, recreation, and so on. Some of the results were highly innovative: Columbia will have a system of close-at-hand health-care centers, for example, installed by Johns Hopkins University and emphasizing preventive medicine. The plan for Columbia calls for a cellular arrangement of neighborhoods grouped into villages that are grouped, in turn, into the town. Each cell has a nucleus of community facilities —those of the neighborhood include an elementary school and those of the village, a secondary school—so that facilities used most are closest at hand. Columbia also shows a respect for the natural landscape that is the opposite of the waste and clutter of random development.

It can be accepted as given that the planned new communities would offer an environment superior to that produced by random growth. Beyond this, to assure a high level of public services, the federal government could offer packages of subsidies—other than housing subsidies—tailored to a list of anticipated needs drafted by the development agencies. The principle would be that, if it is asking the new community to take a share of disadvantaged people, the federal government should provide the means of coping with their problems. If the new community is big enough and remote enough to form its own government, the subsidies should go to it (or, while it is being formed, to the development agency); if it is smaller and within existing jurisdictions, the subsidies should go to them.

Something else the new communities must offer is economic opportunity. Here the principle would be not to offer housing for more people than can likely find jobs. New communities built close in, especially smaller ones on leftover urban or suburban land, would be located near existing jobs —adjacent to expanding suburban plants that are straining the local labor supply, for example—or along arteries of commutation. The larger ones farther out would require more elaborate economic development efforts. Essentially, they would have to create much of their own employment base.

The means of doing so would be both public and private. Government cannot mandate economic decisions in the private sector, but it can attempt to influence them. The Advisory Commission on Intergovernmental Relations has proposed that direct federal incentives be offered businesses to locate where growth is desired—in this case, in new communities. The incentives could take one or more of three forms: direct subsidy payments; loans below the market rate of interest; or tax credits on investment in plant or equipment, amount of payroll, or value of products. The commission also has suggested that federal and state governments give preference in awarding contracts to firms that locate where jobs are needed.

Government also can put its own investments to strategic use in the new communities. According to the commission: "Major government installations such as state universities, government office centers, research complexes, military installations, and public works projects can provide a major impetus for growth and can affect the form and character that it takes. Every effort should be made to capitalize on the potential of these major public investments and to realize their multiplier effect."

Not quite every effort is made now. When the Atomic Energy Commission was seeking a site for a $300 million proton accelerator, which eventually will be a magnet for as many as 50,000 persons, it passed over a number of strategic possibilities and chose instead the hamlet of Weston in DuPage County, Illinois—a county that has only 2,000 Negroes out of a population of 500,000, no fair-housing law, and is well beyond the commuting range of the Chicago ghettos. Once Weston was chosen, moreover, no coordinated effort was made by federal agencies to deal with the consequences of the growth that the project will stimulate; in fact, the federal government has no mechanism for doing so. In terms of influencing the pattern of urbanization, the $300 million will be thrown away.

Making jobs available through private and public investment could be a strong magnet for bringing population to the new communities. One more step is required, however, if they are to serve the needs of a segment of the hard-core poor. The new communities should be the staging ground for opportunity. They should offer concentrated programs of job training and supportive services, giving the poor the skills they need to make the most of their new environment. They could thus perform the function that the city once performed for earlier generations of the disadvantaged, but can no longer.

The Money Machine

If stated as a government program, the construction of new communities has a frighteningly expensive sound to it. The scale would have to be enormous to handle any appreciable percentage of the 100 million Americans who will be added to our population between now and the end of the century. But it is not a program. It is, again, *an alternative system for building what we must build anyway*, one way or the other. And it contains a built-in source of revenue that could save the public billions it will otherwise have to spend.

The revenue would be created through the process of converting land into development sites: the manufacturing, in the Douglas Commission's term, of urban land ready to build upon. Land on the edges of metropolis, where most of the new-community building would go on, is often priced at or near the level of farm acreage. When it is made ready for development by the installation of roads, utility lines, and other services, the value soars.

As previously noted, the investment that makes the land developable is mainly public. The profit from the jump in price is entirely private, and usually winds up in the pockets of speculators. A system of public land acquisition and resale would return to the public the profit from its investment. Now hear this testimony from William E. Finley, the man in charge of planning Columbia and a hard-headed habitual reader of the balance sheets of urban development: The profit gained from conversion of rural to urban land values would be sufficient, says Finley, to pay all of the public agency's costs in seeing to the planning and development of a large new community, including the installation of public facilities— and there would be something left over at the end.

The British experience gives clear corroboration to Finley's statement. Wyndham Thomas, who heads the development corporation that is undertaking expansion of the city of Peterborough from 80,000 to 200,000 residents, offered at an

American conference a detailed financial summary of Britain's postwar new-towns program. All but one of the first eight new towns ringing London earned a profit after about ten years and was able to clear its government loans over the following four to seven years. (The eighth was involved in substantial slum clearance on its site. It, too, is expected to turn a profit eventually.)

If all this has a slightly un-American ring to it, the point should be re-emphasized that very nearly all of the development of new communities under the system proposed here would be in the hands of the private sector. The system would work to the advantage of the private sector, in fact, by assuring a steady supply of developable land at fair prices. The only ones to be disadvantaged would be the speculators and they, putting it bluntly, deserve it.

Land as a public resource becomes incalculably precious at a time of intensive population growth, too precious to remain a commodity. There is no reason on the face of the earth for the public to pay the bill for its plunder. If plunder seems too strong a word, look at the spoiled and sprawling edges of urbanization.

Money aside, for the moment, direct public involvement in land deployment may be the only way to close the wide gap that now exists between our plans and the reality of what is built. Present negative controls have prevented only the grossest of abuses. If the nation wants a better urban environment, it has to take a positive hand in its construction. If the nation wants a single society, it has to build one.

It will not be entirely free. Federal land-acquisition loans can be on a revolving-fund basis, but other forms of federal subsidy proposed above will cost money. There must be additional subsidies, moreover, so that cruel competition will not be created between old and new communities for inadequate funds. But these would be subsidies directed to individuals who have genuine problems, wherever they choose to live. The housing they require, to take the most expensive example, must be built somewhere; it is not a net addition to the bill, past due and payable, for the nation's so-far unmet needs. The assistance that would go to the low-income residents of new communities will be required, whether or not new communities are built.

To some the above proposals will seem remote from the tragedy of the slums and ghettos, irrelevant, a cop-out. Yet some such change in the system by which the nation is built is essential if the degradation of the slums and the confinement of the ghettos are to be eliminated. To be a single society we have to find places where some of us, black and white, can live together, get to know each other, begin to work things out. Under present patterns of residence, which the present system continually reinforces and replicates, we cannot even take the first simple step of starting school together: Without a change in these patterns, desegregation of the schools in the city is not going to happen; jobs, especially entry-level jobs, are not going to make a massive counter-migration to the city; housing will stay blighted so long as the people in it have no other place to go. The building of new alternatives could open the way to the rebuilding of the city, so that its residents would have the choice of staying, or leaving, without the penalty of life in a destructive evironment.

9

Local
Democracy

New Yorkers, with their characteristic blend of pride and masochism, like to tell visitors that their city is ungovernable. New Yorkers are inclined toward overstatement, but in this case they err, if at all, on the conservative side. The fact is that no major American city, as presently structured, is governable if governance is defined as coping with civic problems.

The principal reason relates to what architects call scale— the right fit of size to function. City government, paradoxically, is at once too small and too big to cope. It is too small to deal with those problems, the majority, that extend beyond its jurisdiction into the thicket of metropolis. Air pollution is one such problem, stubbornly refusing to stop on either side of the city limits. Similarly, adequate open space to soothe the city-frayed nerves is to be found, and preserved, on the metropolitan fringe, out of the city's legal reach. A transportation system worthy of the name must be interurban, must link the city and its more or less interdependent suburbs.

These are environmental problems, but city government also is too small to cope with its deep economic and social malaise. When wealth leaves for the suburbs, the city's tax collectors cannot follow. When the poor come, the city must give them sustenance and shelter them in towers. It cannot build them places to live beyond its boundaries, where the work and the land are.

On the other end of the paradox, city government has grown too big to be as directly responsive as many of its citizens would like it to be—and as some demand that it be. City hall seems remote and unreachable. Reform has taken away the bosses and ward heelers, once a link between city hall and the neighborhoods, and inserted in their place vast, anonymous layers of administrators and bureaucrats. Bigness makes every problem that much more difficult to solve. The Upjohn Institute is in the midst of studies that indicate that the costs of city government increase *geometrically* with size. There is every reason to postulate a similar progression of citizen frustration and discontent.

Efforts to correct these discrepancies in scale have so far proceeded separately and without too much success. The good-government answer to city government's smallness is metropolitanization: extension of the city's jurisdiction to match the boundaries of metropolis and, thus, the boundaries of the city's major problems. Early in their growth several big cities—San Francisco, Denver, Philadelphia, New York—were consolidated with their counties in an effort to achieve this match. In the past generation, Nashville, Baton Rouge, and Jacksonville have followed suit. Miami and its suburbs delegated some powers to Dade County and seem ready to delegate more. Indianapolis is the latest city to try partial metropolitanization; it was installed, by popular vote, in early 1969.

But voters in Cleveland, St. Louis, Richmond, and elsewhere have turned it down. Opposition has mounted around the country, to the extent that many urban political scientists are convinced that metropolitanization is, for the foreseeable future, a pipe dream. Metro, as the extreme conservatives call it, is regarded by a vocal few as being, quite literally, a Communist plot to weaken local independence. It is a special threat to suburbanites who see it, with some accuracy, as a means of opening the gates to all those people with all those problems they moved away from. The militant blacks, for their part, look on metropolitan government as a device for keeping power in white hands as the black populations of the central cities grow. Lest they be thought paranoid, it should be pointed out that at least some of the advocates of metropolitanization in Indianapolis openly argued from the rise in black political power, pointing out that the added numbers of suburbanites were needed to keep the whites in power. Atlanta, for many years, has had an interesting history of annexing new (white) territory with each increase in the city's black electorate.

In the absence of metropolitan government, the device commonly used to deal with metropolitan problems is the special-purpose authority or district. The map of metropolis is crisscrossed with such districts, established to operate parks, cemeteries, and zoos, to eradicate mosquitoes, to build sewers and tunnels and bridges. Each has its own board and staff— and its own singular concern. Neither the boundaries nor the agendas of these districts often match, which means that related problems—transportation and open space, for example —are considered in grand isolation from one another. The directors of these districts, moreover, often are appointed rather than elected, and thus are free of accountability to the citizens. Some, such as the New York Port Authority, attain legendary power and wealth and can do with it just about what they please.

A recent movement to untie this tangle has been the spread in metropolitan areas of the so-called Councils of Governments (COGs). The COGs are composed of mayors, county supervisors, and other locally elected officials of the governments that make up metropolis. The movement began in Detroit, in 1954, but did not gather momentum until a decade later when the federal government introduced requirements for regional planning and offered to help pay for it. The COGs were designated as one means of carrying out the planning and receiving the federal aid. Since then they have been formed in well over half of the metropolitan areas in all parts of the country.

They have grown in strength as well as in number. The first COGs were little more than luncheon clubs, allowing the local officials to get to know one another by their first names. With the federal planning assistance came the need to make some decisions that would be binding on the governments represented around the table. In a few areas—San Francisco, the twin cities of Minneapolis and St. Paul, Washington— this decision-making power has been extended beyond planning to development, and COGs also are beginning to take their first tentative steps toward consideration of social problems.

The particular utility of the COGs is that they allow local officials to consider common problems in relation to one another, in contrast to the special-district approach. Also, these officials are at least indirectly accountable to the voters of metropolis through their own local elections. The other side of this coin, however, is that their hearts remain with the voters in their own jurisdictions; the political rewards come from protecting local interests, not from sacrificing them to a larger good. The COGs, according to the director of one of the most active of them, can be "no stronger than the political courage of their weakest members." That does not make them very strong, but they are, at this moment, the best means of metropolitan problem-solving that we have.

Back in the city, the fight against bigness and for responsiveness is taking two directions. One is toward decentralization of the decision-making powers and delivery systems of city government. The other, advanced by a coalition of frustrated blacks and white theorists, would amount to an *ad hoc* secession of minority neighborhoods from the city.

The latter proposals usually call for some form of neighborhood corporation as the vehicle. Milton Kotler, of the Institute for Policy Studies, who helped organize the pioneer East Columbus (Ohio) Community Organization, has called for federal aid to be channelled directly to such corporations, bypassing city hall as well as the state house. W. H. Ferry of the Fund for the Republic has suggested that these corporations be the basis for coexistence between "blacktown and whitetown," with "Blacktown, Incorporated," making the decisions and whitetown offering resources without strings and, except when asked, without advice.[1] The Community Self-Determination Act essentially was designed to encourage such multipurpose community corporations and to establish a national corporation to provide them with public and private support.

For all the surface appeal of these proposals, they rest on some fragile and potentially harmful premises. The likelihood of white resources being provided in sufficient quantity without strings has already been questioned. ("The major difference between the ghetto and the rest of America is that its residents are effectually outside the economic machine," writes Ferry, who then proposes, in effect, that their exclusion be institutionalized.) But there are other, more fundamental problems, beyond even the obvious one that the devices proposed by Ferry and others would carve the city, and society, into permanent racial colonies. The substitution of corporations for government in the black neighborhoods could have the effect of disenfranchising those residents who do not share the separatist outlook. "Let them choose their own leaders," says Ferry, but many of the leaders of the neighborhood corporations established to date have been more-or-less self-appointed or put in power partly by whites. Spokesmen for some groups bent on black self-determination have made it clear they desire to be the appointed, not the elected, leaders of the ghetto. Witness Kermit Scott, of CORE, who stated, at a 1968 seminar on black entrepreneurship, that it was insufficient to say that the people in the ghettos should make their own decisions. "That kind of so-called democratic process is not enough at this point," Scott said. "We have to eliminate that just as it has been eliminated for now in many underdeveloped countries."

Even if an electoral process to choose corporation leaders

were installed, it would have the effect of cutting the city up into overlapping and, to the voter, confusing jurisdictions; it is already happening in some cities that hold special elections for Model Cities, anti-poverty, health, and other program districts. The map of the city could become as chaotic as the map of metropolis is now. Solution of city-wide problems could become all but impossible, as solution of metropolitan problems is now.

The more promising alternative is structural decentralization of city government itself. It was the choice of the Civil Disorders Commission, which proposed a two-stage process beginning with the creation of "neighborhood action task forces." Composed of both neighborhood residents and city officials, including representatives of the mayor, such task forces would attempt to coordinate delivery of services by city agencies and would function as "community cabinets" to identify and act upon neighborhood needs. The second stage would be transformation of the task forces into neighborhood city halls complete with some decision-making powers, left unspecified by the commission. Alongside the city halls would be one-stop neighborhood centers dispensing federal, state, and city services.

The response to the commission's proposal has not been overwhelming. Only a few cities have taken steps in this direction, and they have been tentative steps. Mayor Ivan Allen of Atlanta set up government-community task forces in six problem neighborhoods and also, as a resource to them, a city hall task force of all relevant agencies. Community-service officers were stationed in neighborhood centers to listen to complaints and get action on problems at an early stage. Dan Sweat, the mayor's assistant who set up the system and made sure that city agencies delivered, is pleased with the results. "Citizens now know where to go for what," he says, "and we know who to go to in the neighborhoods."

New York's Lindsay, vice chairman of the commission, tried to establish neighborhood city halls early in his administration but was refused funds by the Democratic-controlled city council. He subsequently opened five, called "neighborhood action centers," with foundation grants and other private contributions. Each was staffed round the clock to give advice and provide access to officials who could solve problems. Lindsay also established twenty task forces of city officials to work in their spare time in storefront offices staffed by neighborhood residents.

Boston's little city halls were established by Mayor White as part of an Office of Public Service, which also runs a round-the-clock telephone complaint center and performs various coordinating roles among city agencies. There are ten little city halls in operation and three more planned. Most are in portable trailers that cost $5,000 to buy and furnish and are staffed by an average of six city employees. One, in Boston's South End, also has a full-time federal social security representative, a health clinic, a library, recreation facilities, and fourteen housing inspectors. In their first six months of operation, these little city halls handled more than 5,000 written complaints and requests for services, plus an uncounted number that came in by person or telephone.

Most of the requests involved the bread-and-butter services of city government. The little city halls function much as the ward bosses' offices once did, and there is evidence that they are gradually changing the neighborhood residents' feelings about their government. The Irish working-class community of Charlestown at first wanted no part of the little city halls program. After seeing them in operation elsewhere, 2,000 Charlestown residents petitioned Mayor White for one of their own.

They are also changing, if slowly and gradually, the ways of the city bureaucracy. The little city hall staffs feel personally responsible to the neighborhoods they serve. They become neighborhood advocates and push city agencies for response. They are not always successful, but Daniel J. Finn, head of the Office of Public Service, points to "a day-by-day lessening of the obstinate refusal by department workers to do anything." The fact that Finn is known as "the mayor's man" helps.

James Breay, a young psychiatric social worker who is Finn's deputy, sees in the program the prospect of more city employees moving out of the main city hall and into those in the neighborhoods. In the process, he hopes, they will become "generalists instead of specialists. If so, it could mean new civil service classifications. In other words, we could write specs for a brand new category of civil servants, so no one would be sitting at his desk with nothing to do, going home early."

So far, Boston's little city halls program remains an experiment. It needs to be expanded, refined, and replicated in other cities—fast. With increasing urgency and decreasing patience, the residents of the cities' troubled neighborhoods are insisting that their voices be heard and heeded. If the structure of city government is not remodeled, partially rebuilt closer to these people and their problems, they may one day decide to take it, and society, apart.

Levels of Response

Local government's dual discrepancies in scale are firmly linked. The same system that allows 20,000 people in a suburb substantial control over their civic destiny—allows them to create their own exclusive environment and the world be damned—denies 20,000 people in an urban neighborhood any effective role in shaping the institutions that shape their lives.

The means of removing these discrepancies also must be linked. Control of one's destiny cannot be taken away from the suburban resident at the same time that it is being given to the city dweller. Full-blown metropolitan government, by itself, would only give to both a diluted franchise, spreading the sense of remoteness from the center of power. Decentralization of city government, by itself, would only redistribute an insufficiency of power, sharing more widely the incapacity for dealing with problems that are metropolitan in scale.

It is possible to combine elements of the two—metropolitanization and decentralization—into a kind of metropolitan federalism. This would require, first, sorting out the problems of metropolitan living according to scale, and, second, seeing that there is a level of governmental response appropriate to each. These tasks could keep political scientists and special commissions busily at work for years; what follows is a generalized set of suggestions as to how they might be approached.

There is obvious need, as a starting point, for a metropolitan governmental entity to handle problems of the shared environment: those involving air and water resources, area-wide transportation systems, large-scale open space and recreation, and major utilities. It would be similar to the present COGs in its scale and multiproblem focus. But its functions would include development and operations, as well as planning, in the problem areas listed above. It would have taxing powers, and its members would be elected directly by the voters of the entire metropolitan area.

The special districts and authorities with jurisdiction over these problem areas would be dissolved, but all existing local governments would be left intact. They would retain jurisdiction over local concerns such as schools, libraries, social services, police and fire protection—over anything not specifically ceded to the metropolitan agency or council.

In only one area beyond large-scale environmental concerns would the metropolitan agency have the right to intervene in local decisions, and that would be housing. If it could show that local zoning or other regulations were being used for exclusionary purposes, thus fostering racial and class concentration elsewhere, the metropolitan agency would have the authority to supercede these regulations and see that housing was built where needed. In particular, it would use this authority in cases where new employment centers are remote from housing that their workers, at every level, can afford.

The second major need is for a new governmental entity at the neighborhood level in cities that grow beyond a specified size. It, too, would be elective and would be the recognized body to represent the neighborhood in any program requiring citizen participation. It would, in fact, be given broad authority to decide how neighborhood-improvement funds were to be used, within standards of performance and equity set by the general city government. Each neighborhood would contain an outpost of the general government to coordinate delivery of city services and to act as liaison with the neighborhood council.

There are endless forms this new structure might take. The heads of the neighborhood councils, for example, might automatically sit on the city-wide governing body. A similar linkage might be established between local governments and the metropolitan agency; the latter could have a bicameral system combining officials elected locally and area-wide. However they are achieved, the essential objectives of the redesign would be to distinguish between local and metropolitan concerns, matching each to its own politically accountable jurisdiction, and to give the presently underrepresented residents of urban neighborhoods explicit powers over the decisions that shape their lives.

Working it out would require compromises all around. Contributions of power would be required of city hall and the suburbanites. The blacks, for their part, would be receiving an immediate share of power in the neighborhoods but trading off some of their potential power as likely inheritors of city hall where they are, or are approaching, a majority. Possibly their most significant gain would be access to a power ladder—from the neighborhoods to city government to the possibility of influencing decisions on a metropolitan scale. This last possibility is presently closed tight against the blacks, as it is to other city dwellers, a fact that contributes heavily to keeping them down.

The compromises won't come easily. New York City's wrenching struggle over school decentralization shows how painful and divisive the transfer of power can be. Many of the parties involved, moreover, have a strong stake in the present system. It will take equally strong incentives to move them to accept, or cease resisting, change.

One such incentive could be fear. The present governmental chaos in metropolis is demonstrably contributing to urban tension. What encouragement has been given the poor and the minorities in their drive for control of their own destinies may have opened Pandora's box—but it is not likely to be closed again without, alternatively, change or civil warfare. The New York school situation is worth watching in this respect. The state legislature desired mightily and obviously to turn the clock back to predecentralization days and, in its 1969 session, contrived a school law for the city that was ingeniously unworkable. Residents of the neighborhoods that have tasted decentralization face a tortuous time continuing it under this law. No one doubts they will try—and that the result will be a whole new round of confrontations.

Another incentive could be dissatisfaction. No one, not even the suburbanites, is well served by the present condition of the metropolitan environment. The promise of easing traffic jams, cleaning fetid air and foul water, and generally making life a little easier and more pleasant could lead the suburbs to delegate some of their power. Similarly, the growing unease of white city dwellers, the feeling that government is cold to their needs, could lead them to support measures to make government more directly responsive.

The largest incentive of all, however, could be money. Local government, as noted earlier, is strapped; local property taxpayers are burdened beyond all equity. No substantial progress of any kind is going to be made until more money comes back from Washington. If an element of national urban policy were the restructuring of local government, this could be the most significant string placed on the federal money as it passes back down to the places where people live.

10

Priorities

Beyond all oratory, the proprietors of government indicate what they think is important, and what they think is not, by where they spend the public's money. This is where they chose to spend it in fiscal 1969, according to Bureau of the Budget figures:

Program Area	Amount (in billions)	Per Cent of Total
Total federal spending	$202.2	100.0
National defense	81.7	40.4
Health and welfare	55.0	27.2
Interest payments	17.0	8.4
Commerce and transportation	9.1	4.5
Veterans	8.2	4.1
Education and manpower	7.9	3.9
Agriculture	5.2	2.6
Space	4.0	2.0
International	4.0	2.0
Natural resources	3.7	1.8
General government (housekeeping)	3.6	1.8
Community development and housing	2.8	1.4

What these figures seem to indicate, on their face, is that our national leaders, though mightily concerned with America's military position in the world, are still compassionate toward citizens in need of assistance in areas such as health, welfare, education, and employment. What they conceal is the degree to which federal money is diverted from those whose need is greatest into a variety of enterprises whose priority, at this time of foreign and domestic trouble, is unsupportable.

The seemingly large investment in the health and welfare category, for example, includes Social Security and other self-fed trust funds for which the government acts as little more than a public insurance broker. These funds make up nearly 80 per cent of the $55 billion allocated to health and welfare programs in fiscal 1969. The education and manpower category includes only one major program—Title I of the Elementary and Secondary Education Act of 1965—that is specifically directed to the needs of school districts with concentrations of children from low-income families. Title I accounts for $1 billion of the total, and this billion is diffused by the congressional standards that make eligible *any* school district containing ten poor children—not 10 per cent but ten individuals, regardless of the district's size and over-all wealth. The manpower portion of this item, roughly $2 billion, includes some $300 million for federal support of the state employment services, notorious for their laggardness in attending to the needs of the hard-core jobless. The commerce and transportation category contains approximately $5 billion for federal highway aid—or nearly twice the total budgeted for all community-development and housing programs. And so on, item by item.

The games that can be played with the budget's big round numbers are endless, and many were refined, if not invented, by the Johnson Administration. Senator Ribicoff, during his hearings, persistently tried to get from Administration witnesses the total of federal dollars being spent on the cities and their disadvantaged people. Secretary Weaver estimated $28 billion, which the Senator flatly refused to believe. Attorney General Nicholas Katzenbach came in at $13 billion, but the Senator noted that this total included "such things as payments to states and counties from grazing receipts."

By the Budget Bureau's tabulation, the fiscal 1969 budget provides $16 billion in federal aid to the governments of metropolis and nearly $28 billion in assistance to the poor, wherever they live. Accepting these figures, and the fact they are the highest in recent budgetary history, they still represent 8 per cent and 13 per cent, respectively, of total federal spending. This—by the most generous computation—is the level of importance the components of domestic crisis have attained in the minds of our national political leaders.

The numbers above reflect only front-door federal spending. Enormous amounts also go out the back door (or, perhaps more properly, fail to come in the front in the first place) through tax exemptions that reduce federal revenues. Many economists argue that this lost revenue should be considered an expenditure, just as surely as if it had been collected, budgeted, and paid out. Among them is Stanley Surrey, former Assistant Secretary of the Treasury, who spent two years constructing a "tax-expenditures" budget that, for fiscal 1969, added up to $46 billion.[1] The priorities revealed by this second federal budget are even more drastically warped than those reflected in the first.

Surrey followed the categories of the regular budget, and his largest was health and welfare. His total for this category was $15.6 billion, a figure that was reached only by the inclusion of the $3.2 billion going to taxpayers who chose the standard 10 per cent deduction instead of itemizing. Precious little of the remainder, moreover, went to the poor. Extra exemptions for the aged, for example, amounted to $2.3 billion. Because the more one earns, the larger is the amount of one's exemptions, the largest share of this seemingly benign reverse outlay goes to couples with incomes over $200,000, the smallest to persons earning between $1,600 to $2,000, and none at all to those with incomes below $1,600, according to Brookings Institution economist Henry Aaron, who was a consultant to Surrey. Aaron commented that the workings of this set of exemptions, which amount to a large-scale public-assistance program, were "so bizarre . . . that one can hardly imagine any public figure introducing it," at least not through the front door.

Under the category of community development and housing, Surrey found that property-tax and mortgage-interest deductions to homeowners amounted to a tax expenditure of $3.95 billion. The benefits, of course, go mainly to the property-holding middle and upper classes, and the larger the holdings, the larger the benefits. The total is very nearly double the housing and community-development items in the regular budget, the only items that help shelter those of low or moderate income. Planner Charles Abrams has for years described our system as "free enterprise for the poor and socialism for the rich," and the Surrey budget makes his description sound less like an epigram and more like a basic truth.

It also gives a hollow ring to the pleas of those, notably including the present President and his predecessor, who say that the nation cannot afford to do more for the cities, the blacks, and the poor. Their argument, of course, has been that in wartime the nation cannot buy both guns and butter, at least not without disastrous inflation. But there is an additional, unspoken premise to this argument. They are actually saying that the nation cannot afford both—*and do its business as usual.* They accept the general shape of both federal budgets, direct and indirect, as givens.

Money could be found to do much more even within the butter category of the direct budget. The point was demonstrated in a 1968 report by the Committee for Economic Development, an organization composed not of mayors or black-oriented leaders but of the highest level of businessmen and educators.[2] CED began its examination by dividing federal nondefense expenditures into "new" programs, those that seek "the reduction of poverty and improvement of the conditions of urban life"; and "old" programs, those that "serve the purposes of an earlier day, purposes which must surely decline in the relative scale of national priorities as other values rise." Under new programs, it included housing and community development; health, labor, and welfare; and education. Under old, it put space research and technology; agriculture and agricultural resources; natural resources; commerce and transportation; and veterans benefits and services.

The CED report then placed expenditures for new and old programs side by side for the fiscal years 1960 through 1969, excluding lending authorities and insurance trusts. In 1960, $5.8 billion was spent on the new programs, by CED's reckoning, and $14 billion on the old. By 1966, with the Great Society getting underway, it was $11.6 billion for the new and $23.3 billion for the old. In 1969 budget estimates, it was $19.9 billion for the new and $26.6 billion for the old. Spending for the new programs had increased markedly, but still remained about a seventh of the national budget, by CED's measurement. Spending for the old programs had increased more gradually but nonetheless steadily.

"These older programs, by and large, serve useful functions," the report said. "Nevertheless, it is seriously to be questioned whether in the light of our current scale of national values continued expenditure on them in excess of $25 billion a year can be justified." It then bravely proposed:

1. "A slowdown in the space program and some shift of scientific and managerial talent to the solution of the more critical problems of the cities." The space program, the report said, "acquired its present ambitious goals at a time when there was fear that the country was deficient in 'national purpose' and 'challenge' to enlist our energies and uplift our spirits. But everyone now recognizes challenges and purposes on the ground, at home and abroad, which abundantly occupy our attention as well as our resources."

2. "Sizable cuts in the $4.5 billion expenditure for agriculture [later increased in the actual budget] most of which goes for subsidies." The agriculture item has continued to grow "despite a 25 per cent increase in real net income per farm and a 20 per cent decline in the farm labor force in the

past five years," the report pointed out. "There should be a vigorous push for modernization of these programs whose intellectual and political roots were in the entirely different world of 30 to 50 years ago."

3. "A more substantial stretchout than the President [Mr. Johnson] has proposed in the program for reclamation, rivers, and harbors." There was $1 billion in the budget estimates for such projects, to which CED politely avoided attaching the traditional appellation "pork barrel."

4. "Postponement of highway expenditures along the lines of the President's proposal plus some redirection of this spending toward higher benefit-to-cost highway projects. This change will permit a shift in construction activity toward urban construction projects that are urgently needed."

CED noted that in these four recommendations it had not exhausted all possibilities for cuts in not-so-essential programs. The Defense Department budget is "not sacrosanct," it said pointedly. The most encouraging phenomenon of the early Nixon months, in fact, may have been the emergence of strong voices in Congress willing to question defense spending. Foreign policy is not within the competence of this book; the point is, these voices were being raised in the name of budgetary sanity as well as of peace. For years, even the McNamara years, there was suspicion that the Defense Department budget contained a far higher fat content than found in anyone's butter, but the friends of the military in Congress intimidated the suspicious and kept the billions coming.

Now the suspicions are being publicly confirmed. A single example: The first Nixon defense budget contained requests for development of three new types of aircraft that Andrew Hamilton, national-security editor of the new *National Journal*, has estimated would cost $30 billion to build over a ten-year period in quantities sufficient for their intended missions.[3] Yet, Hamilton argued persuasively, existing models would do to meet the predictable need for manned flying forces in an age of missiles. The $3 billion per year, Hamilton pointed out, could

> nearly double federal support for primary and secondary education; or double federal job and training programs for the unemployed and disadvantaged; or nearly double the present level of federal public assistance (income support) grants; or triple the present level of food assistance programs to combat hunger; or provide nearly 20 times the present level of federal assistance for urban mass transportation.

Similarly, the significance of the Anti-Ballistic Missile controversy, in terms of the domestic emergency, is that it is a preview of the great post-Vietnam priorities fights that are certain to come. The Defense Department already is telling Congress that, when the war ends, its budgetary needs won't dip more than $10 billion (just as the spacemen, having found the moon a giant sandbox, are attempting to generate national enthusiasm for going on, in the 1970's, to Mars). The giant defense and space suppliers are showing little interest in domestic markets. It is hard not to view the ABM program, given all the scientific-military challenges to its worth, as a welfare program for the military-industrial complex when an end to war diminishes its markets.

Some of the corporate recipients sat in a Washington ballroom the day after the President announced his intention to build the ABM system. The occasion was a meeting of the job-generating National Alliance of Businessmen, and one of the speakers was Richard D. Hatcher, the black mayor of Gary, Indiana. "It would be superficial, I think, to view yesterday's decision on the ABM as solely a presidential decision," Hatcher said. "For whether you care to admit it or not, you— the men sitting in this room, those who occupy the seats of power in the major corporations of our country—participated in that decision. You did so by a heady infatuation with defense contracts and an unreasoned fear, I think, of facing a peace economy. Even if, as predicted, the ABM were only to cost $7 billion, we have denied to our society almost 400,000 hospital beds, or 18,000 elementary schools, or 700,000 low-rent apartments." Hatcher concluded, "You have helped to make this system and you must help now to humanize it." He sat down to polite applause, and other speakers continued to praise NAB's employment record and exhort it to do more.

During the cold war years, there grew up in this country a tacit tradition that priorities analysis stops at the water's edge. Decisions about ABMs and aircraft are measured against our commitments to maintain peace and freedom in the world, and domestic undertakings must be scaled to what is left over within the further limits of what the tax-paying public can (or will) bear. In the process, the "new" programs of aid to the cities, the blacks, and the poor—new because these needs have risen so tardily in the national consciousness—are especially vulnerable. They have yet to develop powerful, identifiable constituencies in or out of government. If the residents of the slums and ghettos are last hired and first fired, the programs that serve them are last to be funded and first to be cut.

The spending of every federal dollar should be measured against the same standard of national need. That standard should be set in recognition of the immediate danger to national security contained in the division and distress that centers in the cities. For what will it profit the nation to work and spend to achieve peace and freedom in the world, only to see them die at home?

Past Due and Payable

The nation has lived for centuries on the patience of the poor and the minorities. In recent years, the bill has been passed to the cities, who have been expected to meet rising needs and demands with declining revenues. Now the poor and the minorities are less willing to pay with their labor and deprivation for the affluence of others. The cities are unable even to meet their day-to-day housekeeping obligations. America, as a nation, must decide whether it will assume the price of freedom now or pay later to clear the rubble of its dreams.

The price, in part, is a redistribution of private and public income. Poverty cannot be eased, much less eliminated, without some transfer of individual wealth from the top of the income scale, where it remains concentrated, to the bottom, where it remains pathetically scarce. At the end of World War II, the top 20 per cent of the population earned 43 per cent of the total personal income; two decades later, its share is 41.2 per cent. The bottom 20 per cent, in 1946, earned 5 per cent of the total personal income; its share now is 5.4 per cent.

The history of compassion, of humanity, in this country can be read in its efforts to change this ratio, efforts that began slowly at the beginning of this century, spurted with the New Deal and the war, and have become all but dormant with the postwar quest for individual affluence. Economic progress in this sense, rather than as recorded in the GNP, has resulted largely from the intervention of the national government. This intervention has taken two forms: changes in the rules of the economic game, such as the legitimization of the labor movement; and increased taking of funds from the haves, through taxation, and giving to the have-nots.

The Great Society represented this second form of intervention, but it was stalled by war and social conflict. It is past time for another try. This time, however, it must get further from the New Deal model. There must be a redistribution of publc, as well as private, income to end multiple crises of the cities.

It has been historically true in America that humane purpose has been most successfully achieved at the national level of government. It probably remains true, despite the recent behavior of Congress and the growth in the responsiveness, under fire, of big-city mayors. The leverage to move the country to meet the needs of the poor, the minorities, and the cities remains in Washington. That is where the public money goes. That is where the responsibility lies: Poverty and prejudice, the prime creators of the slums and ghettos, are national rather than local problems.

Yet there is less truth to the corollary, at least implicit in the New Deal and later efforts at reform, that wisdom also is centralized in Washington. This kind of thinking, for decades the baggage of liberalism, has led to the creation of thick layers of bureaucracy set up to protect federal funds from their users out there beyond the capital, layers that often act as barriers between programs and their purposes. There are sincere government reformers who even now regard movements toward self-determination on the local level as a new conservatism that gets in the way of federally directed progress. The lesson that *how* federal funds are spent is at least as important as *how much* has not, in Washington, been universally learned. Uncle still knows best.

Sometimes he does. Stripping federal aid to education of safeguards against its use to maintain segregation, for example, would scarcely improve the situation of the blacks. Allowing urban-renewal funds to be used for downtown shopping malls does little to house the poor. For years this was allowed and the cities did use the funds this way, indicating the nature of their own priorities.

It is, again, a matter of scale, the fit of power to purpose. Large national objectives, such as the creation of a single society, must be built into federal programs in the form of binding requirements for the general use of the money. It is proper for the federal government to direct that urban-renewal funds enlarge the housing opportunities of the poor. What is obtrusive is for the federal government to wrap the funds in a maze of small requirements concerning every detail of a project's execution. Flexibility, and imagination on the part of local communities and local governments are to be encouraged. That means, as a start, that they must be permitted.

What is required is, first, the assumption of national responsibility for national problems, so that the cities, as the locus of many of these problems, would receive a share of federal revenues *as their due*; and, second, maximum use of the leverage of federal funds to increase the responsiveness of state and local government by attaching fewer minor requirements and more large ones linked to over-all national purpose. The two are inseparable: It would not be progress to send the money down unfettered and waste the chance to stimulate change.

The Post-economic City

For change is, above all, what is required—not just in the structure of governments and their budgets but in the very way we think of governments, from Washington to city hall, in relation to ourselves as individuals and communities. The concept of community must be revived and the concept of city redefined in light of change.

"A free society should produce free and responsible individuals as a tree bears fruit," John W. Gardner has written.[4] "That is its purpose." Since the American society is an urban society, that generative purpose devolves to the city, to metropolis. "It should enable the talented to develop their talent," Gardner went on. "It should enable each person to achieve the best that is in him. It should help the lame to walk, and the despairing to hope, and the ignorant to know. It should fight every condition that stunts human growth or warps the mind or dulls the spirit. By doing so, it should make men more free, more responsible, more self-sufficient." Our cities are not functioning this way, and so they yield the strange and bitter fruit of social disorder.

A decade ago—a century in urban history—those who thought at all about the cities tended to blame their problems on the new in-migrants. They were misfits, unused to urban life; the otherwise farsighted collection of *Fortune* magazine essays entitled "The Exploding Metropolis" explained that slum conditions resulted from the "ignorance" of the arriving rural poor about the manners and mores of the city. The view shows up again and again in the sparse urban literature of the 1950's.

It was a comforting view—these newcomers would learn, as others had—but not an accurate one. The in-migrants were better educated, better motivated than those who had grown up in the Harlems of the nation. In part, this was because the act of migration requires both courage and aspiration; it is the most fit who move on. But in greater part it reflected the fact that the city represented, for its minority poor, for those growing up in it, a ruthless environment. It still does. Those already there were being—are being—destroyed. "We very often get the impression that what is wrong with the American city is the Negro, when the reverse is true," Ralph Ellison told the Ribicoff Committee. "What is wrong with the Negro is what we Americans have done to the American city."

Ellison had a suggestion: "I think one of the things we can do about the city is to look at it, not merely as an instrumentality for making money, but as a place for allowing the individual to achieve his highest promise. And with that in mind, try to construct a city, or reconstruct a city, in ways that would encourage a more gracious sense of human possibility."

Only recently have we begun to construct and reconstruct our cities and their institutions with any such intention in mind. Most were built in the full flush of the industrial revolution and were thought of as "both the instrument, and the result, of industrial development," as John Kenneth Galbraith pointed out in a 1967 address to the City Club of New York. The tests of how they were built were "what served economic performance or what resulted from economic development." Most still are being shaped more by laws of the marketplace than by human needs.

The result is what a group of architects once called "the accidental city," built without design or public purpose. Until now, the representative American has been content to let the accident happen. The environment he cares about is his own, bounded by the walls of his apartment or the edge of his lawn. He is disinclined to be concerned about the public places, and the public problems, that he shares with others in his community. He is resistant to spending for community purposes. An axiom of the economic city has been that "what the individual had to spend was good, what he surrendered to the municipality was bad," Galbraith says. "The first was a regard that measured progress to a higher standard of living. The second was a cost that abridged individual liberty."

And so our communities, and our sense of community, have declined as our standard of living has risen. This has been acceptable to most of us, those who share in the general affluence, in the seemingly endless upward curve of individual satisfaction. What is starting to happen now is that the public problems are impinging on our private lives. We smell it in the polluted air that all alike must breathe. We feel it in the epidemic fear and confusion that spread throughout an area struck by civil disorder.

The city will not fulfill its human function, the accident will continue to injure the millions set apart from progress, unless a sense of community is regained. Galbraith suggests that the post-economic city regard itself as "a household with a common and centrally exercised concern for the well-being of all the members." He envisions a city that "will be itself a planning instrument, not merely the reluctant object of the attentions of a planning board. It will have a far larger budget, for its test of service is what improves life, not what minimizes cost. And it will assume responsibility for those who must now look to it for sustenance and well being . . . drawing heavily on the fiscal resources of the national state."

A city, like a household, is a place where people learn to live together; learn to adjust to, perhaps even appreciate, the differences they find in others; learn from others who they are. Without such cities, we will not have a free society.

Epilogue

The times cry for change and the disaffected demand it. Yet our institutions are sluggish, resistant, painfully slow to respond. They were designed for another kind of nation, an earlier societal self-image. Tom Wicker, of *The New York Times*, described the situation in a single sentence in mid-June of 1969. The sentence is complicated, as is the situation, but worth close reading:

> The most powerful nation in the world, with its population shifting inexorably into vast city-states that are little more than political vassals of the 50 political accidents of the federal system; with these jurisdictions further subdivided into mazes of overlapping, inefficient, and jealous units; with a central government that absorbs a lion's share of all the revenues available and thus is responsible for delivering a lion's share of all public services, for most of which it has little aptitude and less understanding—even the most powerful nation in the world, in such circumstances, is simply not organized to do what its ingenuity and resources would otherwise permit.

The blossoms that were on the trees outside the window when this book began have turned to leaves. Today there is a mid-summer storm. The sky is black and thunderous. I wonder if, when the heat rises in the suffocating buildings a few miles away and drives their occupants to the streets, there will be fire with the summer lightning. If I lived on those streets this summer, in a black island of despair surrounded by affluence, by indifference, by aversion, would I counsel hope and patience or join the burning?

I wonder too if a book—words, ideas, exhortations, analyses

175

and policy proposals—can any longer help. Is there time left
to read, to sift and weigh ideas and strategies? Have white
minds hardened to the point where they are beyond penetra-
tion by understanding, by information? Clearly there are two
societies, apart from race: those who want change and those
who resist it. They are widely divergent in their shares of power
—the resistant society remains in charge—and in their views
of what is going on. Students seek identity and freedom, and
Congress considers requiring colleges to adopt institutional
codes of student conduct as a prerequisite for federal funds.
The blacks of Brooklyn seek a role in the operation of their
schools, and the New York State legislature renders powerless
their local boards. The comprehension gap between these two
societies is huge and growing.

It is particularly evident in the behavior of the Nixon Administration. The new President knows who elected him, has
proved he can count. He has not proved that he understands
there are qualities to democracy that transcend electoral math-
ematics—that democracy survives, in great part, through its
capacity to protect the minority from the occasional self-serv-
ing ruthlessness of a majority. If the Great Society was im-
perfect in its readings of, and response to, black strivings in
the cities, the new Administration, in its opening months, has
been coldly remote.

Clearly also there are two time cycles at work. One is the
accelerated cycle of rising expectations, the other the slow-
motion cycle of response and readjustment. Can the first be
slowed and the second speeded before time runs out?

I retain hope. It is based partly on a feeling for the white
middle-class people I grew up among. They shared—I shared—
complicity in the ways that our institutions worked to disad-
vantage the blacks. They viewed America as two societies unequal in abilities, diligence, and accomplishments. This was
a fact of nature, and the exceptions merely proved the rule.
Separation was a corollary: Their experience of the other society was almost nonexistent.

But they were, and are, good people, for the most part kind, compassionate, and, within moral and social limits, tolerant. And as their experience of the other society has grown—if only indirectly, through press and television—so has their understanding and their willingness to see problems, once clearly identified, solved with their tax money. Most of this growth has occurred within the last very few years. It has been limited —vestiges of the old attitudes remain and no great affection has developed for taxes—but it has been noticeable.

I am convinced that if these people knew, really knew, as they do not yet, what it is to be black in the American city, they would respond to the point where national action would be possible. Further, if they were given a persuasive and coherent view of alternative national futures—the threatening consequences of further division versus the promise of a single society—they would choose unity and accept the steps necessary to achieve it. They are also reasonable people, when not in the grip of fear.

My hope also is based on the character of American blacks, who have never been very good haters. No people in history have borne injustice with greater dignity or greater tolerance for their oppressors. It is a tolerance that white Americans have done little to deserve and that is now being eroded. I believe that its restoration would be swift if white institutions showed genuine intention to change.

Black hope awaits rekindling. Joined to the new black pride, given a share of power, it would be an enormous force for bringing about a new society, just and unified, that would better serve us all.

Notes

Chapter 1

1. U.S., Congress, Senate, Committee on Government Operations, Subcommittee on Executive Reorganization, *Federal Role in Urban Affairs: Hearings*, 89th Cong., 2d sess., 1966 and 90th Cong., 1st sess., 1967 (Washington, D.C.: Government Printing Office, 1966, 1967).

2. James L. Sundquist, *Politics and Policy* (Washington, D.C.: The Brookings Institution, 1968).

3. John C. Donovan, *The Politics of Poverty* (New York: Pegasus, 1967).

4. U.S. National Advisory Commission on Civil Disorders, *Report* (Washington, D.C.: Government Printing Office, 1968).

Chapter 2

1. Daniel J. Elazar, "Are We a Nation of Cities?" *Public Interest*, No. 4 (Summer, 1966).

2. Dorothy K. Newman, "The Decentralization of Jobs," *Monthly Labor Review*, XC, No. 5, (May, 1967).

3. Karl E. Taeuber and Alma F. Taeuber, *Negroes in Cities* (Chicago: Aldine, 1965).

4. Kenneth B. Clark, *Dark Ghetto* (New York: Harper & Row, 1965).

5. Lee Rainwater, "Open Letter on White Justice and the Riots," *Transaction*, IV, No. 9 (September, 1967).

6. U.S. Commission on Civil Rights, *A Time to Listen . . . A Time to Act: Voices from the Ghettos of the Nation's Cities* (Washington, D.C.: Government Printing Office, 1967).

7. New Jersey, Governor's Select Commission on Civil Disorder, *Report for Action* (State of New Jersey, 1968).

8. Angus Campbell and Howard Schuman, "Racial Attitudes in Fifteen American Cities," in *Supplemental Studies for The National Advisory Commission on Civil Disorders* (Washington, D.C.: Government Printing Office, 1968, and New York: Frederick A. Praeger, 1968).

Chapter 3

1. Victor H. Palmieri, "An Executive Looks at Private Enterprise and Public Needs," *California Management Review* (Winter, 1967).

2. Oakland Task Force, San Francisco Federal Executive Board, *An Analysis of Federal Decision-Making and Impact: The Federal Government in*

Oakland (Washington, D.C.: U.S. Department of Commerce, Economic Development Administration, 1968–69).

3. Martin Anderson, *The Federal Bulldozer* (Cambridge, Mass.: MIT Press, 1964).

4. Marshall Kaplan, Sheldon P. Gans, and Howard M. Kahn, *The Model Cities Program: A History and Analysis of the Planning Process in Three Cities: Atlanta, Georgia, Seattle, Washington, Dayton, Ohio.* Prepared for the U.S. Department of Housing and Urban Development (Washington, D.C.: Government Printing Office, 1969).

5. Louise Campbell, "Communities: Bedford-Stuyvesant," *City*, II, No. 2 (March, 1968) and No. 3 (May, 1968).

Chapter 4

1. Stokely Carmichael and Charles V. Hamilton, *Black Power: The Politics of Liberation in America* (New York: Random House, 1967).

2. William H. Grier and Price M. Cobbs, *Black Rage* (New York: Basic Books, 1968).

3. Clarence Funnye, "Black Power Conference: The Untogether People: Separate but Gilded?" *Village Voice*, September 26, 1968.

4. Harold C. Fleming, "Analysis: The Unreal Debate Over the Unattainable Objectives of Total Separation or Complete Integration," *City*, II, No. 6 (November–December, 1968).

5. Nathan E. Cohen, "The Los Angeles Riot Study," press release of August 1, 1967 on Nathan E. Cohen *et al.*, *Los Angeles Riot Study* (Los Angeles: University of California, Institute of Government and Public Affairs, 1967).

Chapter 5

1. Murray Friedman, "Kensington, U.S.A.," *La Salle*, XI, No. 4 (Fall, 1967).

2. Robert Coles, "The White Northerner: Pride and Prejudice," *Atlantic Monthly*, CCXVII, No. 6 (June, 1966).

3. Paul Cowan, "Wallace in Yankeeland: The Invisible Revolution," *Village Voice*, July 18, 1968.

4. Nathan Perlmutter, "We Don't Help Blacks by Hurting Whites," *The New York Times Magazine*, October 6, 1968.

5. Bayard Rustin, "The Anatomy of Frustration" (Address delivered at the Fifty-fifth National Commission Meeting of the Anti-Defamation League of B'nai B'rith, held in New York City, May 6, 1968).

Chapter 6

1. Citizens' Board of Inquiry into Hunger and Malnutrition in the United States, *Hunger, U.S.A.* (Washington, D.C.: New Community Press, 1968).

2. Harry C. Bredemeier, "The Politics of the Poverty Cold War," *Urban Affairs Quarterly*, III, No. 4 (June, 1968).

3. Adam Walinsky, "Keeping the Poor in Their Place: Notes on the Importance of Being One-Up," *New Republic*, July 4, 1964.

4. Michael Harrington, *The Other America* (New York: Macmillan, 1962).

5. Charles Silberman, *Crisis in Black and White* (New York: Random House, 1964).

6. John Edgerton, *State Universities and Black Americans: An Inquiry into Desegregation and Equity for Negroes in 100 Public Universities*. Prepared for the Southern Educational Reporting Service (Atlanta, Georgia: Southern Educational Foundation, 1969).

Chapter 7

1. Charles Abrams, *The Negro Housing Problem: A Program for Philadelphia*. Prepared for the City of Philadelphia, Community Renewal Program, December, 1966 (New York: Frederick A. Praeger, 1969).

2. U.S., Department of Labor, *A Sharper Look at Unemployment in U.S. Cities and Slums*, a summary report submitted to the President by the Secretary of Labor, 1966.

3. U.S., Equal Employment Opportunity Commission, *Equal Employment Opportunity Report No. 1: Job Patterns for Minorities and Women in Private Industry—1966* (Washington, D.C.: Government Printing Office, 1968).

4. Samuel M. Burt and Herbert E. Striner, *Toward Greater Industry and Government Involvement in Manpower Development* (Kalamazoo, Mich.: W. E. Upjohn Institute for Employment Research, 1968).

5. U.S., President's Commission on Law Enforcement and Administration of Justice, *Task Force Report: The Police* (Washington, D.C.: Government Printing Office, 1967).

6. James Q. Wilson, "Crime and Law Enforcement," in *Agenda for the Nation*, ed. Kermit Gordon (Washington, D.C.: The Brookings Institution, 1968).

Chapter 8

1. Patricia Leavey Hodge and Philip M. Hauser, *The Challenge of America's Metropolitan Population Outlook: 1960 to 1985*. Prepared for The National Commission on Urban Problems (Washington, D.C.: Government Printing Office, 1968).

2. U.S., National Commission on Urban Problems, *Building the American City*, 91st Cong., 1st sess., 1969 (Washington, D.C.: Government Printing Office, 1969).

3. George W. Schermer Associates, *More Than Shelter: Social Needs in Low- and Moderate-Income Housing*, prepared for The National Commission on Urban Problems (Washington, D.C.: Government Printing Office, 1968).

4. Anthony Downs, "Moving Toward Realistic Housing Goals," in *Agenda for the Nation*, ed. Kermit Gordon (Washington, D.C.: The Brookings Institution, 1968).

5. George Schermer, *Housing Guide to Equal Opportunity* (Washington, D.C.: The Potomac Institute, Inc., 1968).

6. U.S., Advisory Commission on Intergovernmental Relations, *Urban and Rural America: Policies for Future Growth* (Washington, D.C.: Government Printing Office, 1968).

Chapter 9

1. W. H. Ferry, "Blacktown and Whitetown: The Case for a New Federalism," *Saturday Review*, June 15, 1968.

Chapter 10

1. U.S., Congress, Joint Economic Committee, *Supplementary Statement to the Testimony of Secretary of the Treasury Joseph W. Barr: Hearings on the President's Economic Report*, 91st Cong., 1st sess., January 17, 1969.

2. Committee for Economic Development, *The National Economy and the Vietnam War* (New York: Committee for Economic Development, 1968).

3. Andrew Hamilton, "High Flying in the Pentagon," *New Republic*, May 31, 1969.

4. John Gardner, "The Final Answers Lie Within Ourselves: A Plea to All Americans," *Life*, March 8, 1968.